HOMES IN THE EARTH

A DESIGN CONCEPT ASSOCIATES BOOK

LARRY S. CHALMERS A.I.A.   **JEREMY A. JONES A.I.A.**

CHRONICLE BOOKS/SAN FRANCISCO

Book design by Design Concept Associates
Suite 303 N. 14 Howard Street
Spokane, Washington 99201

Chronicle Books
870 Market Street
San Francisco, CA 94102

CONTENTS

	PAGES
INTRODUCTION	5
LIVING WITH THE EARTH	6 – 7
ENERGY	8 – 9
DESIGN DECISIONS	10 – 11
SELECTING AND DEVELOPING THE SITE	12
STRUCTURES	12
FINANCING	13
HILLSIDE HOME	16 – 19
TRUSS-ROOF HOME	20 – 23
TRIANGLE CABIN	24 – 25
ONE-BEDROOM CABIN	26 – 27
BACHELOR PAD	28 – 29
OPEN PLAN	30 – 31
WEST RIDGE PLAN	32 – 33
COUNTRY HOME	34 – 35
MOUNTAIN HIDE-AWAY	36 – 37
DIAGONAL ROOF	38 – 39
TUNNEL HOME	40 – 41
NARROW N.-S. PLAN	42 – 43
COURT ENTRY	44 – 45
TWO-WAY PLAN	46 – 47
EAST ENTRY	48 – 49
TRADITIONAL HOME	50 – 51
PATIO HOME	52 – 53
WEST-VIEW HOME	54 – 57
TWO WING HOME	58 – 59
PAVILION HOME	60 – 61
THREE-BEDROOM HOME	62 – 63
FOUR-BEDROOM HOME	64 – 65
BEACH CABIN	66 – 67
MOUNTAIN RETREAT	68 – 69
SECOND STORY ENTRY	70 – 73
ATRIUM HOME	74 – 77
SPLIT-LEVEL HOME	78 – 79
NORTH-VIEW HOME	80 – 81
STEP CONDOMINIUM	82 – 85
SLOPE CONDOMINIUM	86 – 89
TWO-LEVEL CONDOMINIUM	90 – 91
TWO-STORY CONDOMINIUM	92 – 93
SNAIL PLAN	94 – 95
THREE-CURVE PLAN	96 – 97
THREE-CIRCLE PLAN	98 – 99
SEMI-CIRCLES PLAN	100 – 101
CIRCLES PLAN	102 – 103
SYMBOLIC CIRCLE PLAN	104 – 107
ATRIUM-MOUND PLAN	108 – 109
RADIATING PLAN	110 – 111

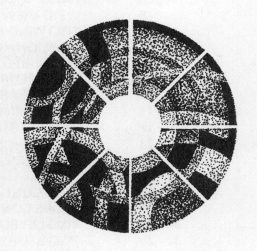

DESIGN
CONCEPT
ASSOCIATES

INTRODUCTION

Earth-sheltering is a principle rather than a style. It is the reduction of energy consumption by minimizing heat exchange rather than by applying devices. It is the saving of energy by not requiring it in the first place.

Recently many publications have announced "types" of subterranean houses or attempted to show the proper way to shape the facade. It is the intention of this book to display a sufficiently large number of designs to demonstrate that earth-sheltering suggests as many forms as it inhibits. As with any other form of housing, the design should support a chosen lifestyle rather than dictate it.

Some of the designs in this book were produced for clients and others border on fantasy but all could be built. In most cases there would be several construction options depending on site factors, available labor and materials, and many other variables. It is our hope that the designs shown in this book will inspire still other thoughts in readers, for their own homes in the earth. Permission is given to all other architects, designers, and builders to use any of the ideas and plans in this book under their own responsibility. However, publication rights for all graphic material are reserved.

LIVING WITH THE EARTH

Architecture includes the design of places as well as buildings. A common theme among many designs which have withstood the test of time is the integration of site and building. Sometimes there is no choice. More recently the use of color and plane has been used to make a merely symbolic reference to setting as Frank Lloyd Wright did with horizontal "prairie" lines. Earth-sheltering extends the bond of building and site directly rather than abstractly in a manner as devoid of fad and cliche as the wildflower and the pine tree.

In the first half of this century, dominant themes of architectural style (if one believes magazines rather than one's own eyes) converged, forming the "International Style." It was a technological style with minimal elements and responded more to production means than to human needs. Architecture in the 1950s stereotyped this movement as "efficiency" experts sought quantitative and objective solutions to the complex problems of design. Just as the Scientific Method eliminated all factors from consideration except those being tested, design theories minimized the importance of most factors except economy. The theme could be expressed as "man overcoming nature." The whole notion began to crumble when some previously obscure middle-eastern countries began to raise the price of oil. Finally a consideration re-emerged for the place buildings would hold in nature.

Animals, constantly exposed to the elements, are sensitive to changes which people ignore. People have grown so accustomed to controlled environments that their bodies are unable to cope even with changing seasons. They go from artificial autumn in an office building to a sub-zero ski slope in another state for the weekend. Consequently they suffer constant colds and other bodily discomforts. Buildings which orient their occupants to nature help develop awareness, sensitivity, and participation in the ever-changing environment. This does not require a return to primitive conditions or even discomfort — just a change in attitude.

Our new goal should be to use technology to help us live more in tune with natural forces. Noticing changes in the color of leaves, smell of the air, and the phase of the moon does more than make us "nature lovers," it makes us more aware of ourselves and enriches our lives.

Many of the psychological problems associated with modern living are due to the boredom of contrived interiors. There is simply nothing interesting or enduring about most of the spaces we occupy. Design for convenience has meant depletion of natural variation and interest. To counteract boredom, people import a jungle of plants, cover their walls with decorations, and apply ornamentation to the exterior, hoping to make their home resemble a time or place they judge to be more interesting. If the house is an amplification of nature, there can be sufficient interest without arbitrary additions.

ENERGY

Each day energy consumption becomes a more important issue. Power brownouts and blackouts will become an increasing reality rather than a past nuisance. Houses must now be designed so that in a power failure the occupants are capable of maintaining a reasonable level of comfort. This includes keeping warm, preserving food, and maintaining a temporary water supply.

It is now possible to design homes which save energy by not requiring it in the first place. This is the first step in developing self-sufficient homes.

The basic idea of earth-sheltering is simply to take advantage of stable ground temperatures. Average soil temperatures will vary with region, soil type, moisture content, soil depth, and time of year. For much of the northern United States, average soil temperatures ten feet below the surface are 45 to 50 degrees all year. In the middle of winter, when outside air temperatures are far below zero and wind increases the chill factor, an earth-sheltered home will be exposed to unchanging soil temperatures which are sixty degrees warmer. It's that simple. In the summer the earth is cooler than the air so earth-sheltering minimizes the need for cooling. These homes normally have at least one exposed side, usually to the south. Locating the major portion of the glass on the southern exposure traps the sun's rays during the winter months and greatly reduces the heating requirement during sunny days. During long winter nights, the use of insulating drapes or shutters helps lock in heat gained during the day. Glass facing north is detrimental to the energy profile of a house as it loses 7 to 8 times as much heat per square foot as a stud wall (double glazing versus 3½″ batt insulation) while receiving very little solar radiation. All glass should be double pane — it reduces heat loss 40 to 50% compared with single glazing.

Infiltration of outside air, a major cause of heat loss in above-grade homes, is also minimized with earth-sheltering.

In addition to greatly reduced heating costs, properly designed earth-sheltered homes require minimal or no mechanical cooling. This depends on glass area, exposed walls, and many other factors. Any south, east, or west windows should include an outside shading device. Roller shades and overhangs can be designed to block the sun during summer months and then admit light at lower angles in the winter.

Adding 12″ to 18″ of earth on the top of a house with grass or foliage will also keep a house cool in the summer. The advantage of earth on the roof tends to be from reduced cooling requirements, not a good insulator. It can help even temperature from day to day but not over a long period of time.

How far a building is nestled into the ground determines the extent of exposure and consequent heat loss. However, it makes no difference in principle whether the soil is undisturbed or hauled in from miles away. Thus, a mound house with dirt against the walls but not over a highly insulated roof can be nearly as efficient as a comparably sized subterranean home with three feet of dirt on the roof.

The earth acts as a protective blanket surrounding the structure and warms up over a period of several years (approaching room temperature). If the heat source for a home fails, this heated earth mass will resist any tendency toward lowering of temperature, keeping the home comfortable far longer than an above-grade house. With supplemental heat from fireplaces or stoves, warmth can be maintained much longer.

Wood-burning stoves and fireplaces can be a completely adequate source of heat if there is an ample supply of wood. Combustion air should be brought in from outside or the chimney will carry more warmth out of the house than will be radiated into the room. Often a wood-burning heat source can be combined with a furnace fan for air circulation. For some allergic conditions, steady heat and unmoving air seems to be more comfortable.

The selection of heating, ventilating, and air conditioning (mechanical) systems should be thoroughly analyzed to obtain maximum benefits. One system cannot be singled out as being the best for all situations. Analysis should be by a qualified individual (usually the architect's consultant).

If the structure has several interior rooms without operable windows, a forced air system should be considered. This type of system has the ability to circulate the air throughout the entire house to eliminate stale areas. This system can also circulate heat from other sources such as fireplaces. Air conditioning is not always justified, but if it is, a forced air system is necessary.

Large glass areas on buildings in northern climates should have the source of heat or warmed air below the glass to prevent drafts.

Air-source heat pumps have been found to be a good choice for some of the earth-sheltered homes that have been analyzed. These systems are projected to pay back the additional initial cost through fuel savings in about five years. More efficient houses take longer to justify the extra cost. Heat pumps provide heating and cooling whether it is needed or not.

Exhaust systems for bathrooms and kitchens must be part of the mechanical design. There are several methods of exhausting air but planning is required to provide exhaust outlets through the roof.

Complicated solar collectors are not economically feasible at this time for such efficient structures. Storage systems add complications to the home, and the home itself can store much of the energy directly without an intermediary device.

Earth-sheltered housing utilizes a very basic concept of taking advantage of the sun and earth to reduce a home's requirements for fossil fuels and electricity for heating and cooling. The key to design is coordination of these elements with the building structure and mechanical system to develop a single efficient system. This means a simple and reliable mechanical unit which can take advantage of the energy-conserving characteristics of the structure. It requires a building which responds to seasonal changes and natural sources of energy.

DESIGN DECISION DIAGRAM

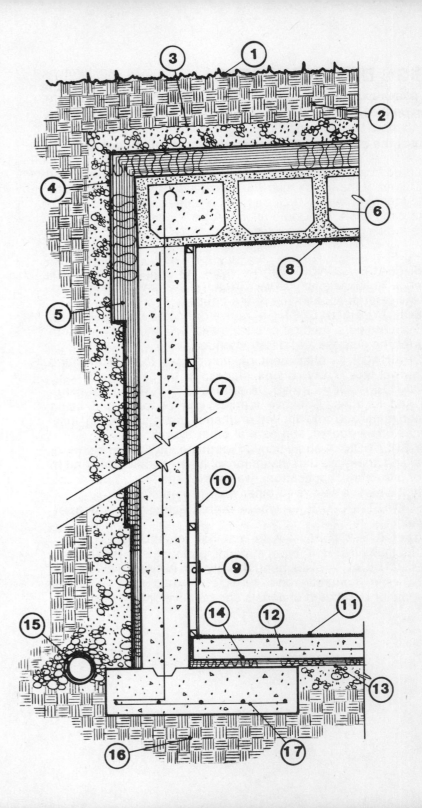

DESIGN DECISION AREAS

Each paragraph below is numbered to correspond to the numbers shown on the DESIGN DECISION DIAGRAM. Many of the numbers apply to more than one location on the diagram. The purpose is to point out the places where a design decision must be made.

1. SURFACE CONDITION — type of foliage, irrigation, resistance to animals, exposure. Often the surface condition provides the exterior appearance of the house.

2. SOIL TYPE AND DEPTH — native or hauled soils, additives, mulches and fillers, method of placement. Soil should be custom mixed for the purpose and depth intended.

3. DRAINAGE — placement of membranes to filter soil and roots, gravel type (if any), drains, slopes.

4. WATERPROOFING AND DAMPPROOFING — type of membrane and location. Effective barriers can be produced using asphaltic materials, cold-applied urethanes, plastic sheeting, clay-impregnated cardboard, and several other hybrid systems.

5. INSULATION — spray-applied urethane, styrofoam board, or mineral and fiberglass batt insulation all have specific uses tied to type of structure, application, waterproofing, and local costs. Usually it's most effective to taper wall insulation.

6. ROOF STRUCTURE — type, material, spans (see structures paragraph).

7. WALL STRUCTURE — type, material, reinforcing.

8. CEILING FINISH — type, material, connections, finishes.

9. ELECTRICAL — placement. Usually it is easiest to place conduit between concrete and furred-out walls, but chair-rail enclosures or baseboard channels can be developed.

10. WALL FINISH — type, material, finish.

11. FLOOR FINISH — type, material, finish. Carpet feels warmer on concrete floors but reduces heat storage. Tile and concrete floors near south windows absorb and slowly re-radiate heat.

12. FLOOR STRUCTURE — placement, ground conditions, material, reinforcement, water treatment.

13. FLOOR INSULATION — insulation such as styrofoam under a concrete floor will help the slab retain heat. In many areas, however, it is not as effective as adding an inch to the roof insulation. It can also isolate the building from the earth heat sink.

14. FLOOR WATERPROOFING — placement, type, application. Often a plastic membrane will reduce moisture rising from the ground. However, this problem should be handled by adequate gravel and footing drains. The plastic barrier can help retain moisture within the slab after pouring and cause a harder cure.

15. DRAINAGE — materials, equipment. In almost all conditions, drain tile or pipe should be placed outside the entire footing wall. For long building shapes and varying floor elevations extra drains should be considered. Usually gravel is also placed under the slab to provide a drainage course for water coming up under the building.

16. SOIL POISONING — required in some localities.

17. FOOTING — shape, placement, reinforcing, size.

SELECTING AND DEVELOPING THE SITE

The site is a major factor in shaping the design of an earth-sheltered home. More sites are acceptable for this approach than for conventional housing, with some exceptions. For example, building in solid rock is expensive initially and less efficient for energy savings.

Site slope is an important element in design but there are more options than most publications suggest. Certainly a "south-facing" slope is an easy setting for passive solar design; however, each compass direction has its own special benefit. With the use of clerestories (high windows) a north slope can accommodate an energy-efficient design. Some of our favorite designs require east or west slopes. Those solve many problems by allowing the slope to pass over the home uninterrupted. Openings are created in the south wall for heat gain and in the north wall for steady light and a second means of exiting. The easiest structure to build is a mound house on a flat side. It offers advantages in drainage, flexibility of plan, and options for windows.

Soil type is critical. Denser soils and rocks are generally more thermally conductive so they are less efficient as "heat sinks" (storing rather than transmitting heat). This can be somewhat overcome by bringing in fill dirt. Clay soils create structural complexities involving expansion and contraction. Layering of soils can channel groundwater, creating drainage problems. Soil conditions should be determined prior to the design of the house and ideally even before the purchase of land.

Other aspects of site selection apply to all types of homes. Location of utilities, drainfields, garages, views, yards, and other items are handled in the same way. Governmental regulations, including setbacks, are usually applied in the same way also.

Rather than looking specifically for a site to fit a design or preconception of the building, we advise clients to find a lot which suits their needs and which they appreciate for its own sake — then design an appropriate house for that site. In some cases we do just a schematic design to help a client realize the extent of land required prior to site selection. We do not, however, design a house and then go looking for a place to put it.

STRUCTURES

Our most cost-effective homes have had concrete walls and heavily insulated standard construction roofs without dirt on them. In most cases this means designing the walls as retaining walls with extra steel reinforcing and then setting the roof directly on top. Where shear is excessive, lugs are extended below the footing. Wood joists or prefabricated trusses are usually used for the roof structure.

It is possible to use treated wood and plywood for earth-covered walls but they provide no heat storage capability and are more complex to detail. Wood retaining walls must be part of a coordinated total design if they are used at all.

Concrete in many forms has provided the roof structure whenever we have placed dirt on the roof except in remote areas. An easy structure to use is concrete plank — usually 12" thick and 4 feet wide — it can span 24 feet with three feet of soil on it. Poured decks and pan joist structures have advantages on larger jobs in urban areas.

Prestressed and post-tensioned concretes have the advantage of developing a camber to cancel deflections from superimposed loads. At first the concrete may actually deflect upwards and then over time start to deflect down due to creep.

Wood roof structures can be used for subterranean houses but they present several problems. First, large beams are becoming harder to find, so either they must be salvaged from demolished structures or glue-laminated beams must be used. Next, the beams must be spaced closely enough together so joists or decking can span the spaces between beams. Finally, allowance must be made for the continuous deflection the beam will make. Other considerations are common to normal wood construction: moisture control, allowances for warping, detailing of joints, and structural connections.

Steel can be used but is not currently cost-effective for residential structures.

FINANCING

For equal sizes, quality, and conditions, earth-sheltered homes cost about the same as conventional homes. Extra structural costs are often made up by lower exterior finish costs. The inside of the house, including utilities, equipment, furnishings, and finishes, does not necessarily differ from that of a regular house.

Each month a homeowner makes a house payment and an energy payment. Savings on energy allow more money to be applied to the house itself.

Loans have been made in the past for subterranean homes and the FHA has approved one of our concepts. H.U.D. requirements, the basis for FHA approval, even begin with site development guidelines which include consideration of existing plants and topography, climate, noise, and maintenance and other factors which are met by earth-sheltered homes far better than by conventional housing. Banks and governmental agencies both prefer to consider plans designed by professional architects and engineers.

NOTES:

40 HOME DESIGNS

The Hillside Home design might be what most people envision as the typical earth-sheltered or subterranean home — rectilinear plan built back into a south-facing hillside and having earth on three sides and the roof. Because passive solar heating was an important design consideration, the windows in the living area were set perpendicular to the winter sun angle to reduce reflection. The angled retaining walls help reflect more warm sunlight inward during winter, while plants cascading down reduce this effect in the summer. In parts of the country where cold but clear winter days are typical, an active solar system could be installed on the fascia panel.

HILLSIDE HOME — 2,000 S.F.

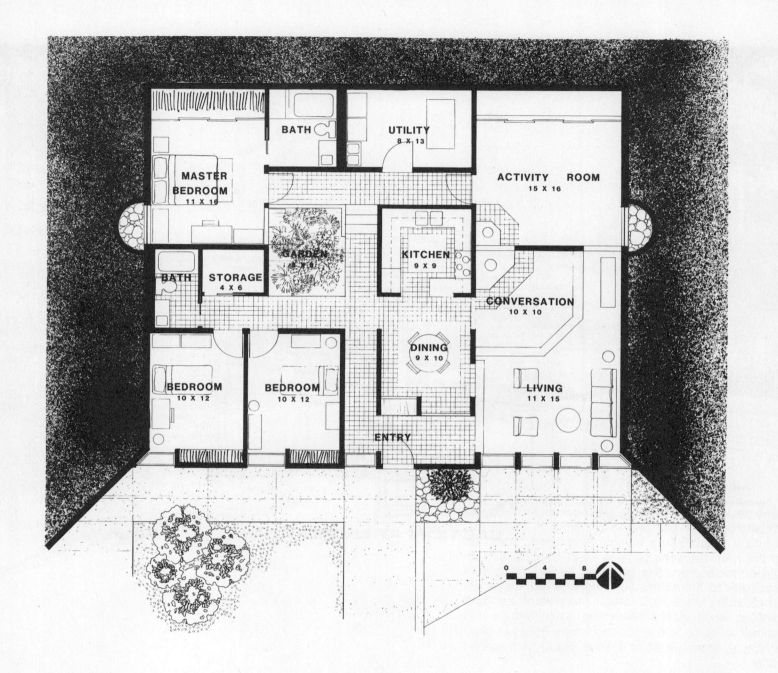

MASTER
BEDROOM
11 X 16

BATH

UTILITY
8 X 13

ACTIVITY ROOM
15 X 16

GARDEN

KITCHEN
9 X 9

BATH

STORAGE
4 X 6

CONVERSATION
10 X 10

DINING
9 X 10

BEDROOM
10 X 12

BEDROOM
10 X 12

LIVING
11 X 15

ENTRY

0 4 8

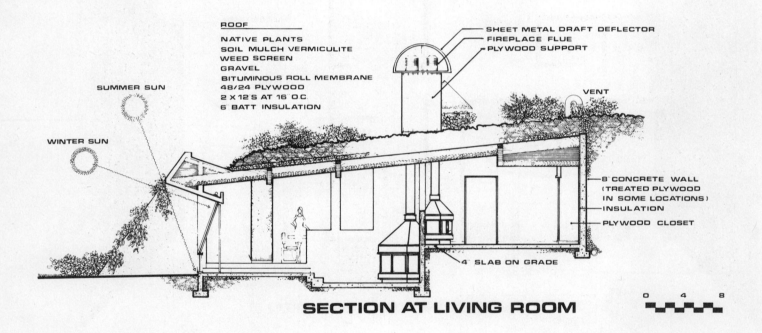

ROOF

NATIVE PLANTS
SOIL MULCH VERMICULITE
WEED SCREEN
GRAVEL
BITUMINOUS ROLL MEMBRANE
48/24 PLYWOOD
2 X 12'S AT 16" O.C.
6" BATT INSULATION

SHEET METAL DRAFT DEFLECTOR
FIREPLACE FLUE
PLYWOOD SUPPORT

VENT

SUMMER SUN

WINTER SUN

8" CONCRETE WALL
(TREATED PLYWOOD
IN SOME LOCATIONS)
INSULATION
PLYWOOD CLOSET

4" SLAB ON GRADE

SECTION AT LIVING ROOM

0   4   8

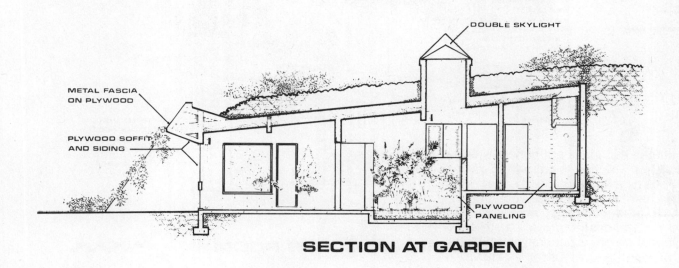

DOUBLE SKYLIGHT

METAL FASCIA
ON PLYWOOD

PLYWOOD SOFFIT
AND SIDING

PLYWOOD
PANELING

SECTION AT GARDEN

The Truss-roof Home demonstrates two ideas not generally associated with earth-sheltered housing. The first is not having dirt on the roof. From an energy-versus-cost standpoint, there is little savings to be gained in many northern states. It takes about nine or more feet of earth on the roof to produce energy savings greater than a well-insulated roof system. The cost to provide a structure for supporting this much additional weight is generally prohibitive. The second idea was to use residential roof trusses as shown in the building section on page 22. Using this standard construction method greatly reduced the cost for materials and allowed the owner to construct much of the home himself. The combination of these two design decisions reduced the energy efficiency an estimated 5 to 10 percent while reducing the cost of construction as much as fifteen percent. The final energy analysis indicates that the truss-roof home should use about 65 percent less energy than its conventional counterpart.

TRUSS-ROOF HOME — 3,360 S.F.

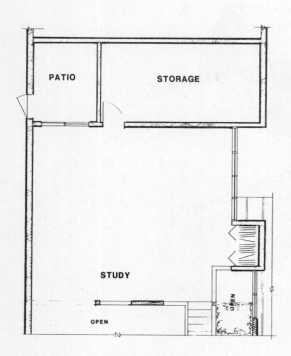

2ND FLOOR PLAN

PATIO

STORAGE

STUDY

OPEN

OPEN

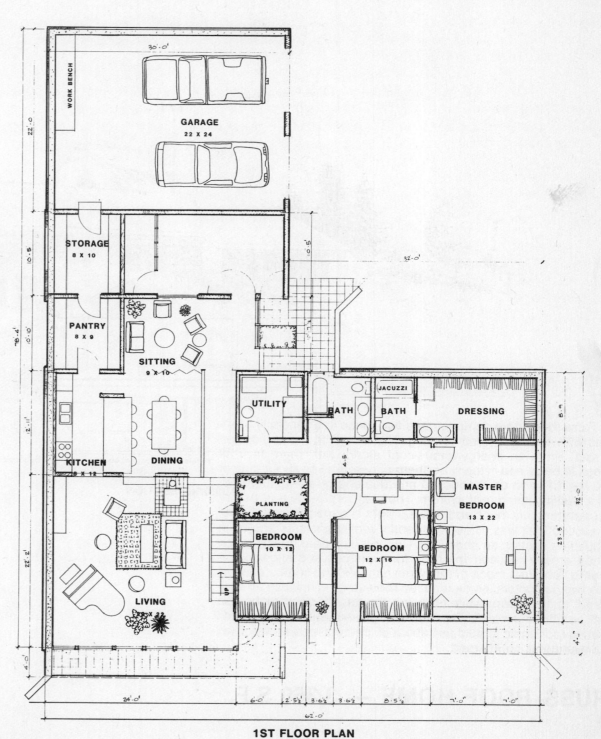

WORK BENCH

GARAGE
22 X 24

STORAGE
8 X 10

PANTRY
8 X 9

SITTING
9 X 10

UTILITY

BATH

JACUZZI

BATH

DRESSING

KITCHEN
8 X 12

DINING

PLANTING

MASTER
BEDROOM
13 X 22

BEDROOM
10 X 12

BEDROOM
12 X 16

LIVING

UP

30'-0"

22'-0"

10'-5"

18'-4"

10'-0"

12'-11"

22'-2"

4'-0"

24'-0"

6'-0"

2'-5½"

3'-6½"

3'-6½"

8'-5½"

7'-0"

7'-0"

62'-0"

32'-0"

10'-5"

8'-9"

23'-3"

32'-0"

4'-5"

4'-0"

1ST FLOOR PLAN

21

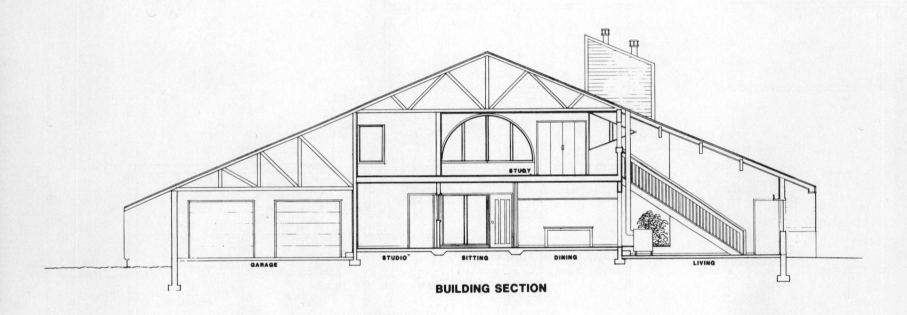

GARAGE   STUDIO   SITTING   DINING   STUDY   LIVING

BUILDING SECTION

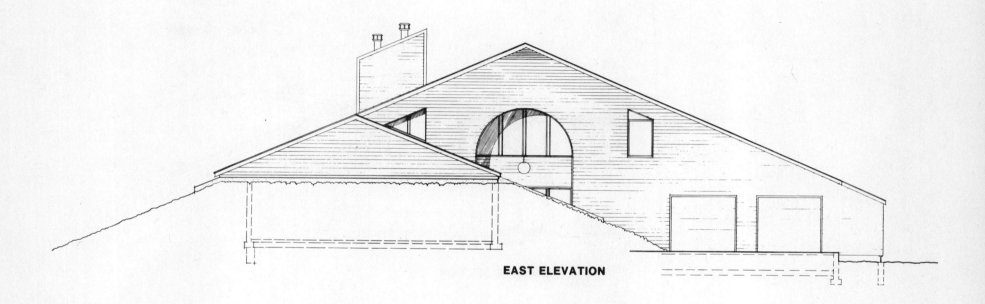

EAST ELEVATION

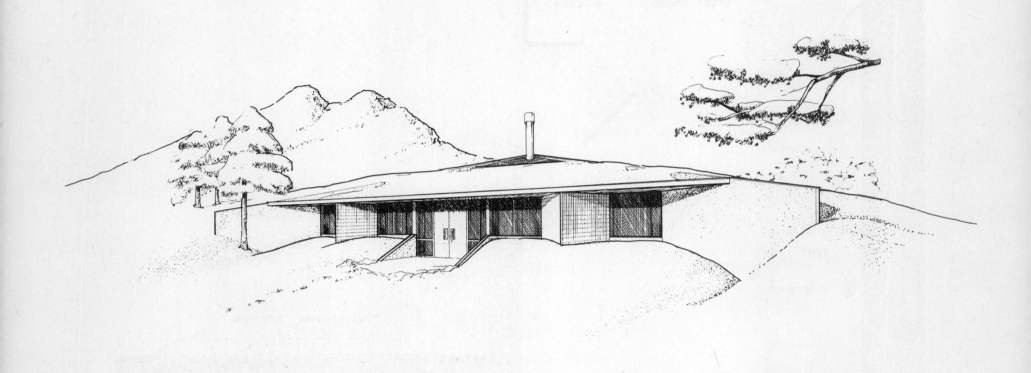

Originally intended as a mountain vacation cabin, this little home is very efficiently arranged with a corner heat source and a wide expanse of southern windows. Although it is ideal for a steep hillside, a similar plan could have a conventional well-insulated roof and beamed ceiling. Two alcoves at the corners form the kitchen and bathroom, and the Murphy bed doesn't need to be pulled down until it's required.

TRIANGLE CABIN — 720 S.F.

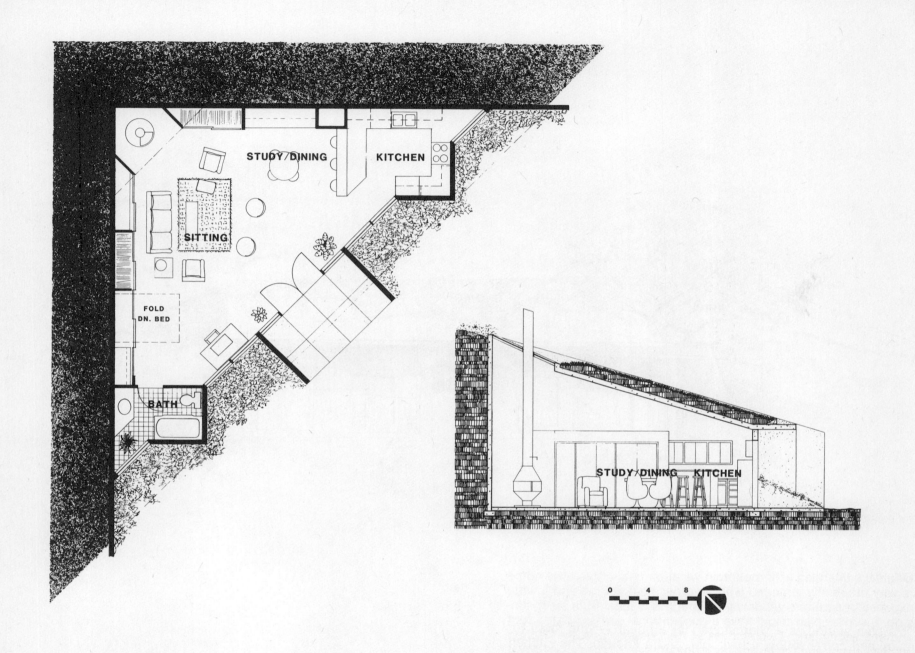

STUDY/DINING   KITCHEN

SITTING

FOLD DN. BED

BATH

STUDY/DINING   KITCHEN

0   4   8

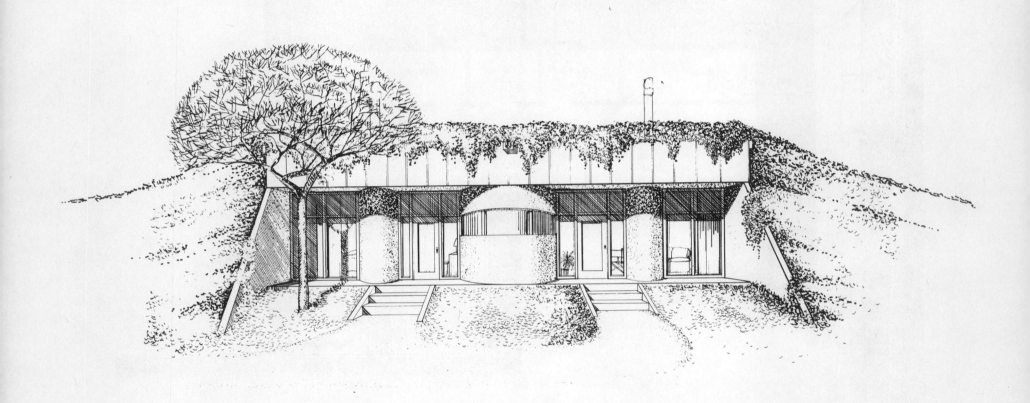

This plan started as a "hermitage" for a priest — one room for study and conversation, a bedroom, and a kitchen. The kitchen wall is bearing to support concrete plank lengthwise on the roof. In another version, the walls flair out to open up to the view.

ONE-BEDROOM CABIN — 900 S.F.

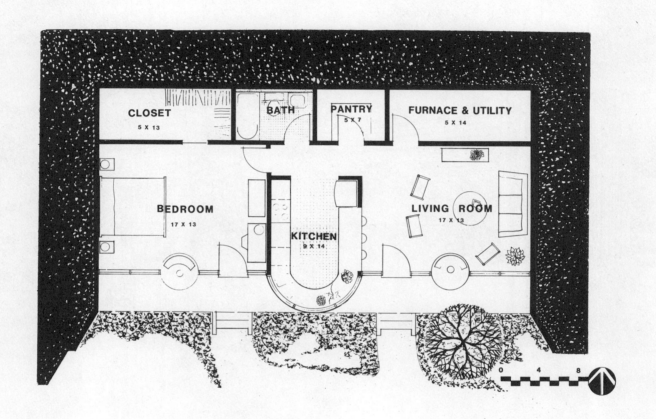

CLOSET
5 X 13

BATH

PANTRY
5 X 7

FURNACE & UTILITY
5 X 14

BEDROOM
17 X 13

KITCHEN
9 X 14

LIVING ROOM
17 X 13

0 4 8

An athletic-facility director wanted a house with the energy advantages of subterranean design but maximum flexibility. In addition, the site is in the flight path of an air base where noise can be a problem. Soil on the roof doubles to reduce noise while saving energy. Only the east and west exterior walls bear a load so that all interior partitions can be sliding screens. The central core contains all of the plumbing. Addition of a deck and trellis provides outside living space and shades the west view into a meadow.

BACHELOR PAD — 1,400 S.F.

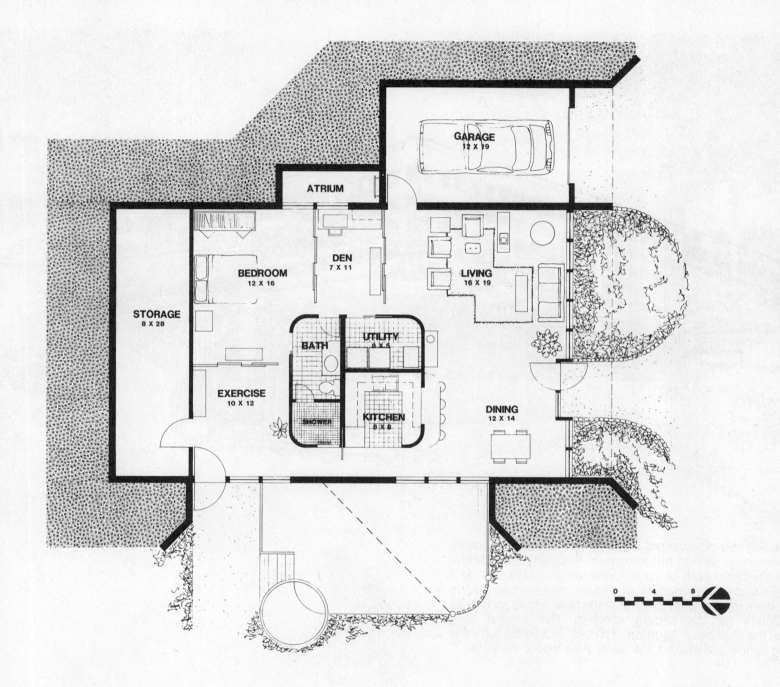

GARAGE
12 X 19

ATRIUM

DEN
7 X 11

LIVING
16 X 19

BEDROOM
12 X 16

STORAGE
8 X 28

BATH

UTILITY
8 X 5

EXERCISE
10 X 12

KITCHEN
8 X 8

DINING
12 X 14

SHOWER

0   4   8

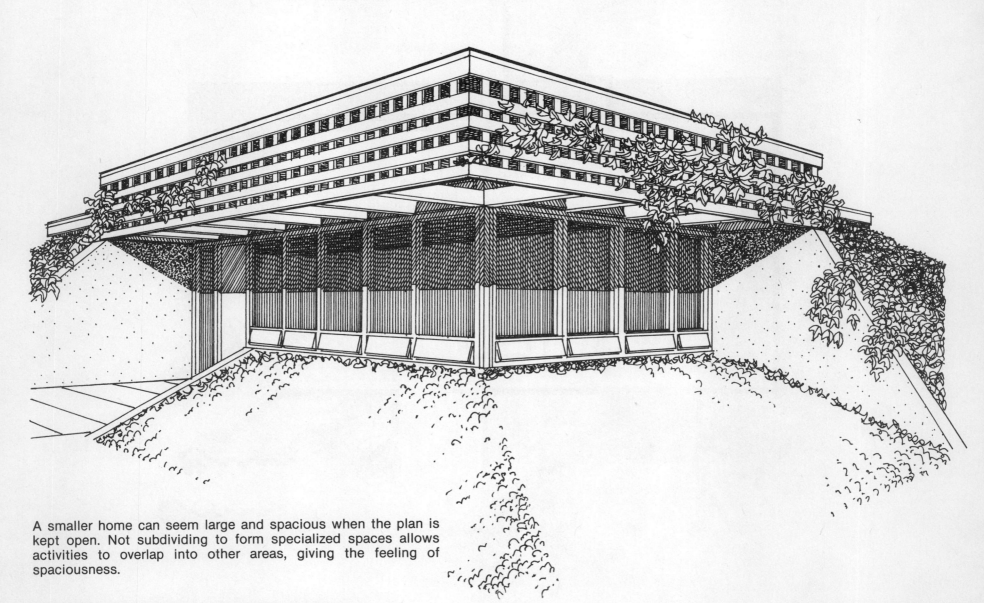

A smaller home can seem large and spacious when the plan is kept open. Not subdividing to form specialized spaces allows activities to overlap into other areas, giving the feeling of spaciousness.

OPEN PLAN — 1,200 S.F.

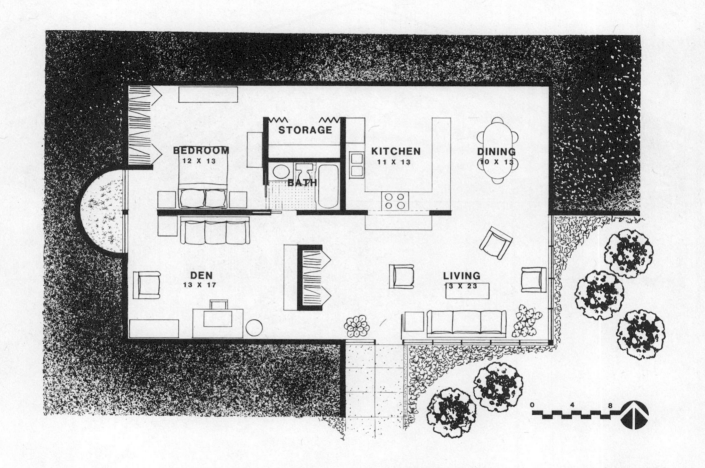

BEDROOM
12 X 13

STORAGE

KITCHEN
11 X 13

DINING
10 X 13

BATH

DEN
13 X 17

LIVING
13 X 23

0   4   8

Instead of a hillside, consider a ridge. This site will have views in two different directions. The owners will have south light for passive solar heating and uniform north light for reading or conducting household tasks.

WEST RIDGE PLAN — 1,680 S.F.

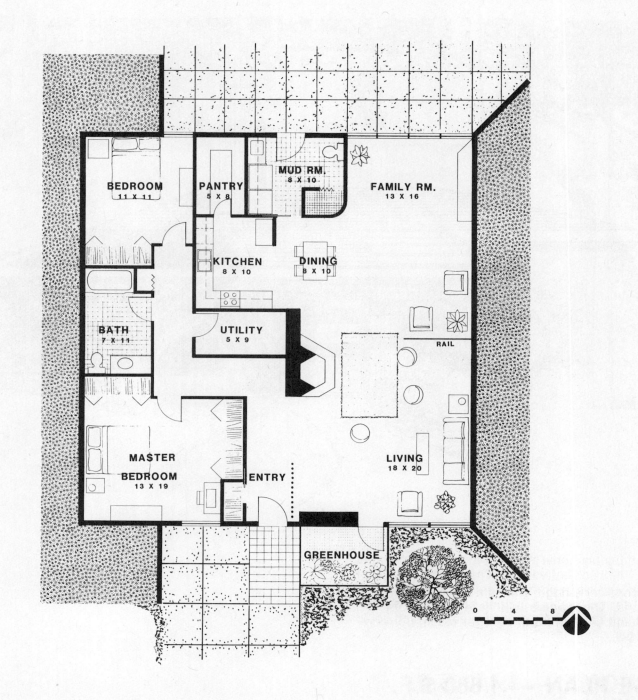

BEDROOM
11 X 11

PANTRY
5 X 8

MUD RM.
8 X 10

FAMILY RM.
13 X 16

KITCHEN
8 X 10

DINING
8 X 10

BATH
7 X 11

UTILITY
5 X 9

RAIL

MASTER
BEDROOM
13 X 19

ENTRY

LIVING
18 X 20

GREENHOUSE

0   4   8

33

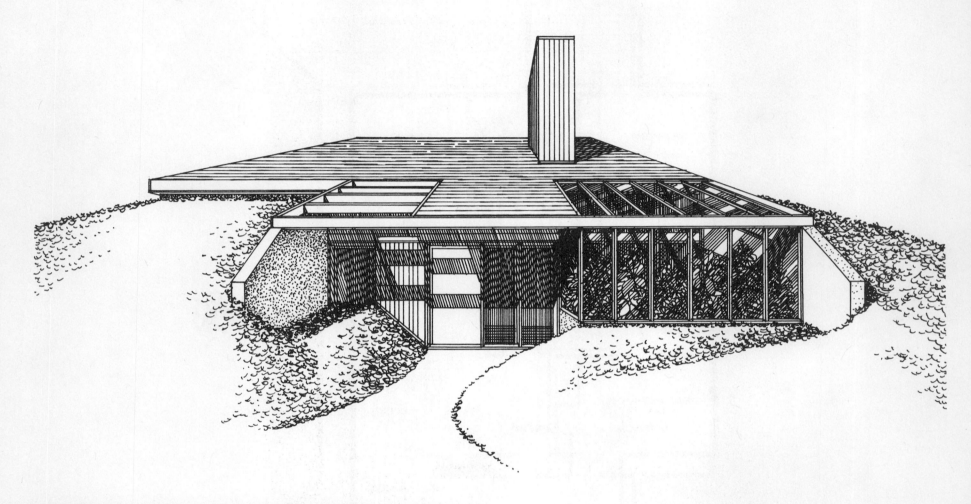

The Country Home offers functional planning for people who work the land they live on. The back entry into the mud room allows for the owners to come in and clean up before setting foot in the rest of the house. Other design features include having the washer, dryer and pantry in one area, creating a service entry which could be located next to a garage or shop.

COUNTRY HOME — 1,440 S.F.

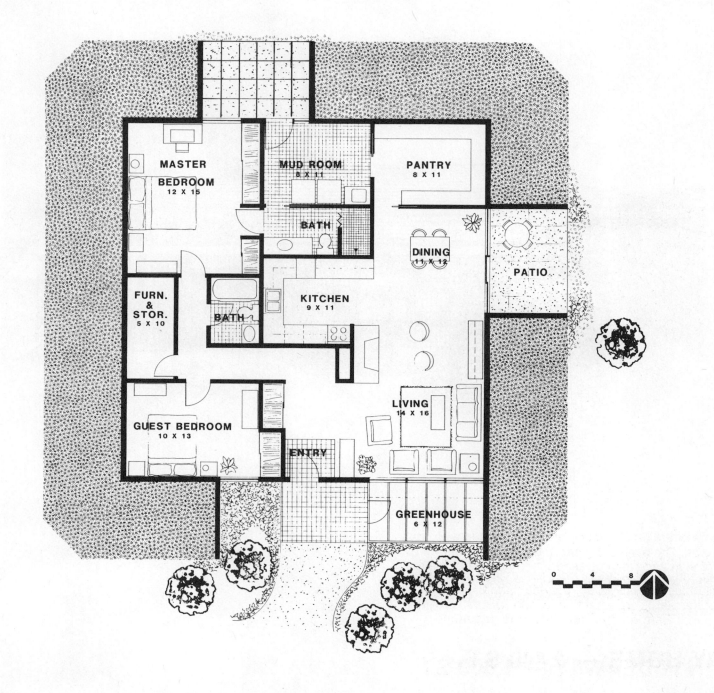

MASTER
BEDROOM
12 X 15

MUD ROOM
8 X 11

PANTRY
8 X 11

BATH

DINING
11 X 12

PATIO

FURN.
&
STOR.
5 X 10

BATH

KITCHEN
9 X 11

LIVING
14 X 16

GUEST BEDROOM
10 X 13

ENTRY

GREENHOUSE
6 X 12

0   4   8

The kitchen is clearly the focal point of this home. It presents itself as the work center and the separation between private and guest areas. The exterior latice and plants will provide natural control for the sun once all of the plants are established, and will also provide the privacy the owners want on their forty-acre mountaintop.

MOUNTAIN HIDEAWAY — 1,600 S.F.

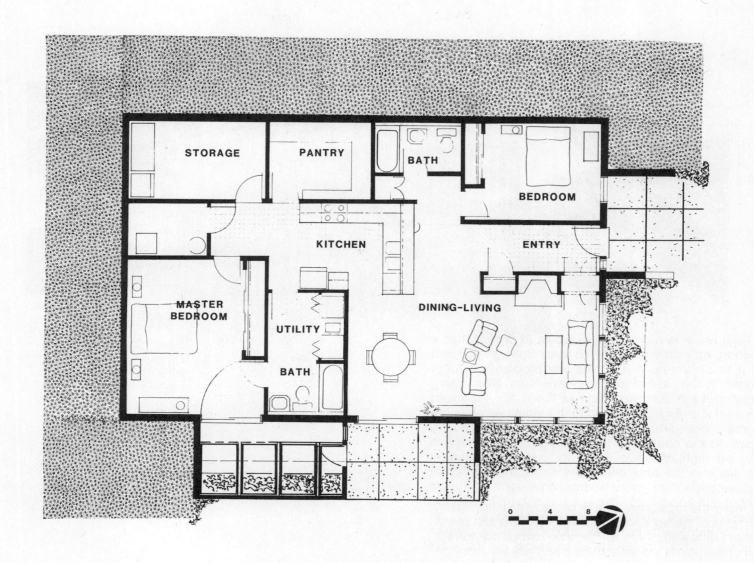

STORAGE

PANTRY

BATH

BEDROOM

KITCHEN

ENTRY

MASTER BEDROOM

DINING-LIVING

UTILITY

BATH

0 4 8

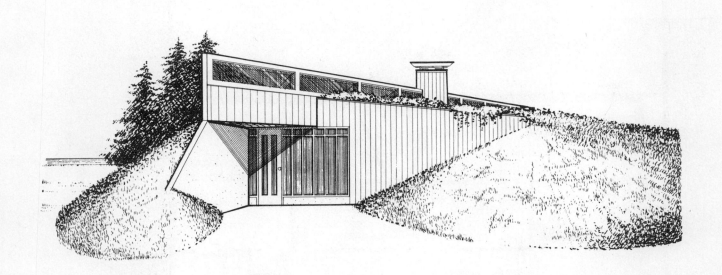

The Diagonal Roof home is more of an exercise in design than a product of function. An architect will often form a design concept and then test it to determine if it solves any problems without creating new ones. In the case of this home we found that raising the roof and having it run diagonally across the space produced several desirable effects. First, it allowed for a higher ceiling in the family, dining and kitchen areas, making them seem larger. It also created windows on the north side for even lighting. With these windows being up high, the possibility for natural ventilation increased. The walls in the area below the lower roof structure were spaced close enough to allow having some earth on top of the house without additional cost. The last major benefit was the creation of a covered entry. For designers, it is essential to find simple design solutions which tie all elements of a project together and solve as many problems as possible for the least cost. .

DIAGONAL ROOF — 1,700 S.F.

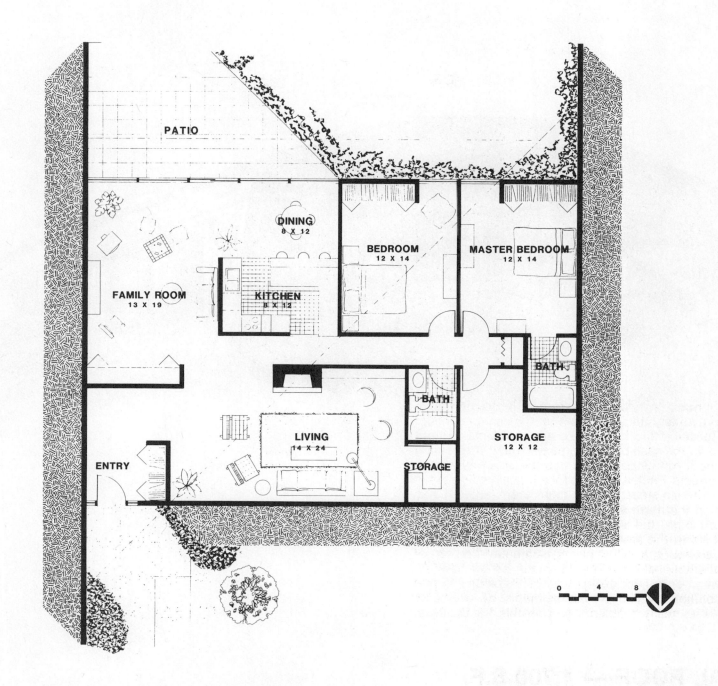

PATIO

DINING
8 X 12

BEDROOM
12 X 14

MASTER BEDROOM
12 X 14

FAMILY ROOM
13 X 19

KITCHEN
8 X 12

BATH

LIVING
14 X 24

BATH

STORAGE
12 X 12

ENTRY

STORAGE

0   4   8

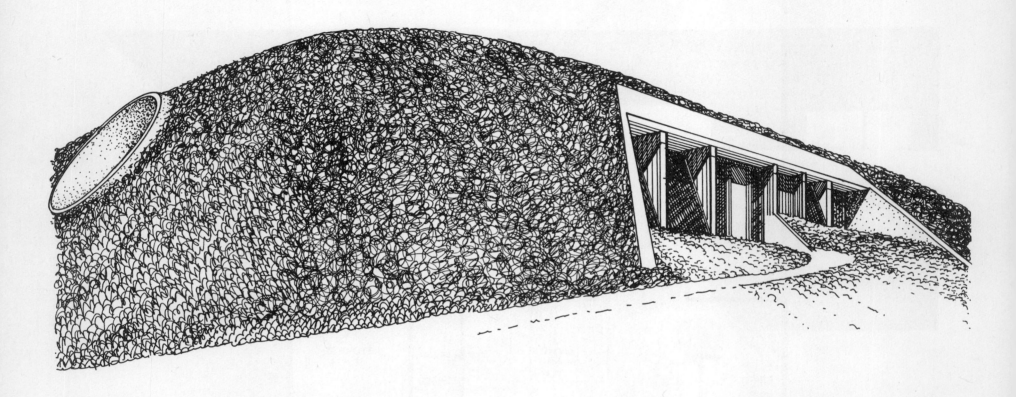

What would it be like to have a corridor (tunnel) eighty feet long running through your home? Could it be functional? Would it be a waste of space? Most of the tunnel area is used for dining and living space and for a gallery. Some of the advantages include the possibility of doing the starter home without the master bedroom and gallery at first. This would provide for lower first cost and ease of adding on. Another nice feature of this plan is that all of the living areas are in the front, with a view, while the utility spaces have been moved to the back.

TUNNEL HOME — 1,770 S.F.

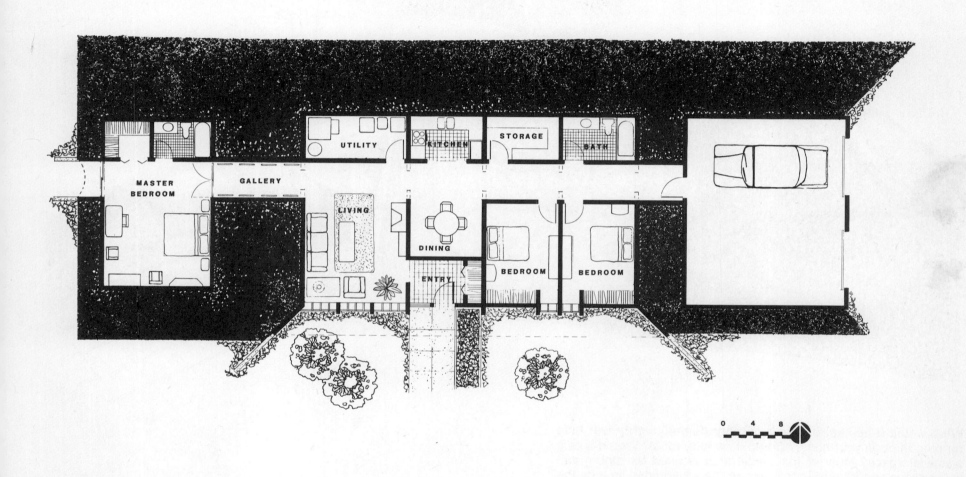

MASTER BEDROOM

GALLERY

UTILITY

KITCHEN

STORAGE

BATH

LIVING

DINING

ENTRY

BEDROOM

BEDROOM

0 4 8

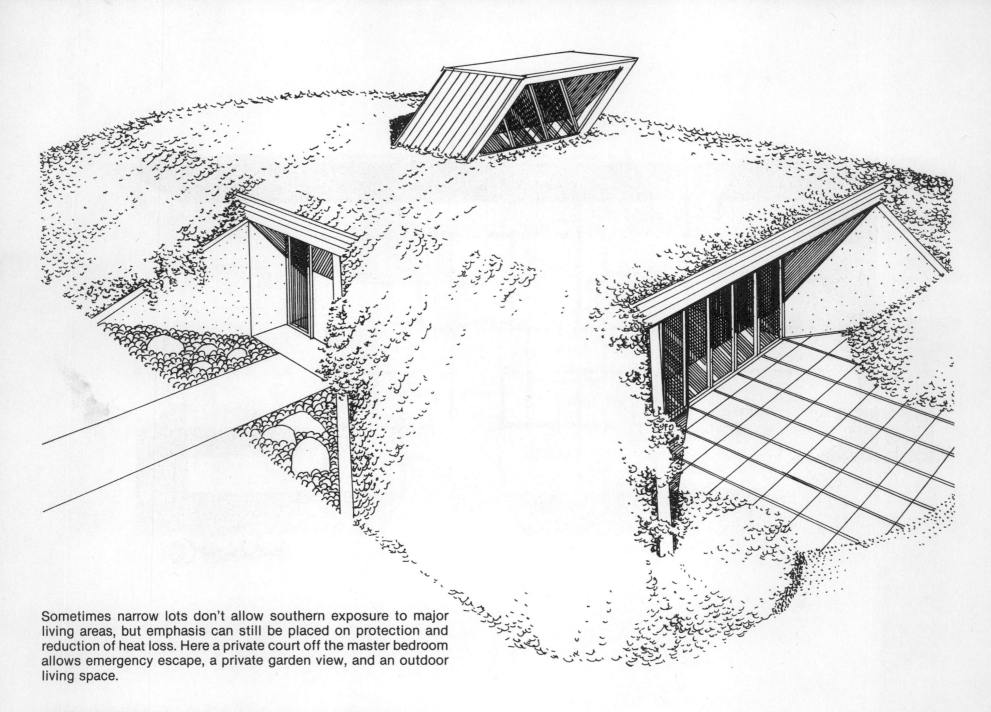

Sometimes narrow lots don't allow southern exposure to major living areas, but emphasis can still be placed on protection and reduction of heat loss. Here a private court off the master bedroom allows emergency escape, a private garden view, and an outdoor living space.

NARROW N-S PLAN — 1,980 S.F.

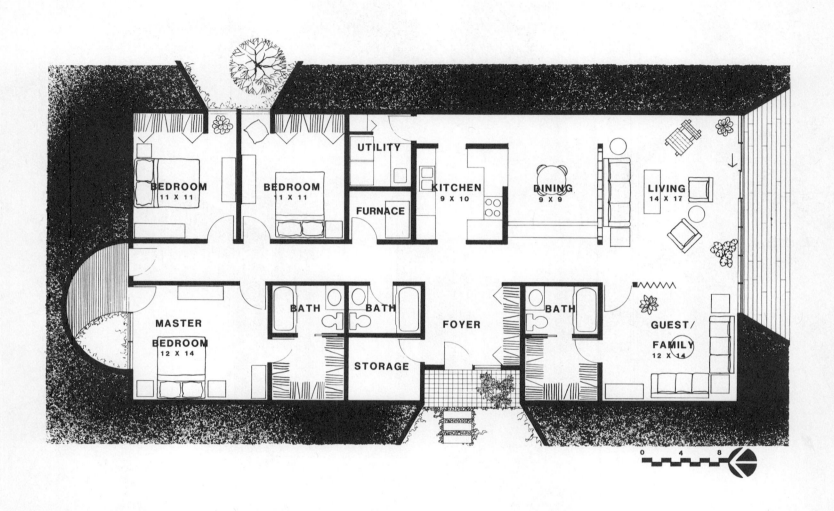

BEDROOM
11 X 11

BEDROOM
11 X 11

UTILITY

KITCHEN
9 X 10

FURNACE

DINING
9 X 9

LIVING
14 X 17

MASTER
BEDROOM
12 X 14

BATH

BATH

BATH

FOYER

GUEST/
FAMILY
12 X 14

STORAGE

0   4   8

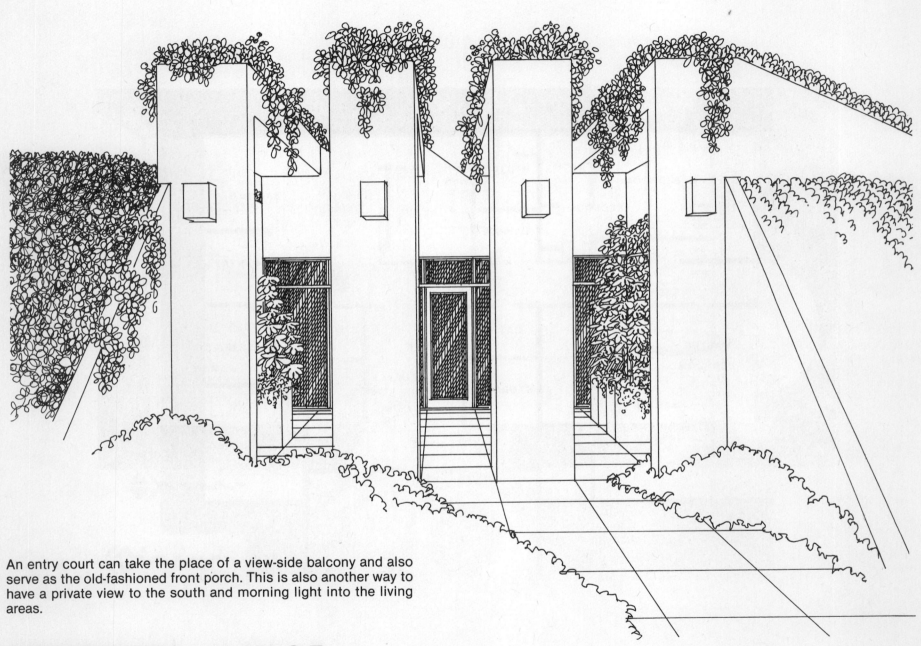

An entry court can take the place of a view-side balcony and also serve as the old-fashioned front porch. This is also another way to have a private view to the south and morning light into the living areas.

COURT ENTRY — 1,560 S.F.

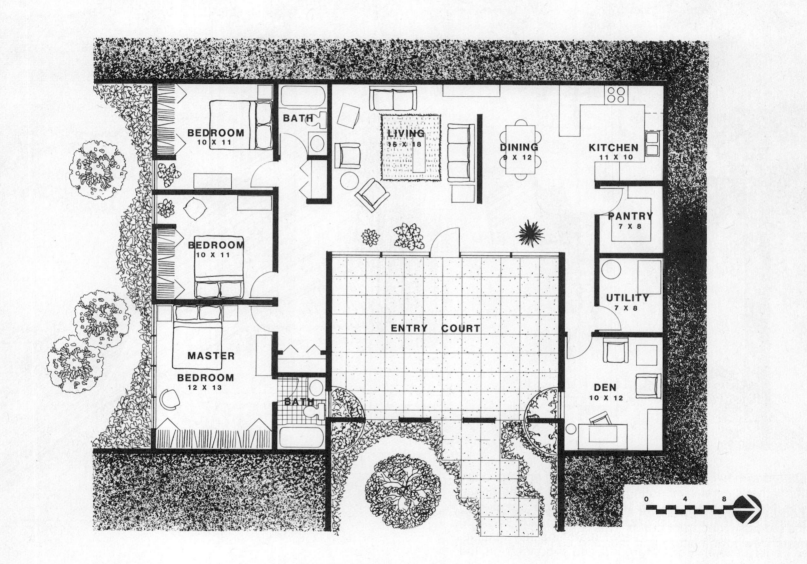

BEDROOM
10 X 11

BATH

LIVING
15 X 18

DINING
9 X 12

KITCHEN
11 X 10

BEDROOM
10 X 11

PANTRY
7 X 8

UTILITY
7 X 8

MASTER
BEDROOM
12 X 13

BATH

ENTRY COURT

DEN
10 X 12

0   4   8

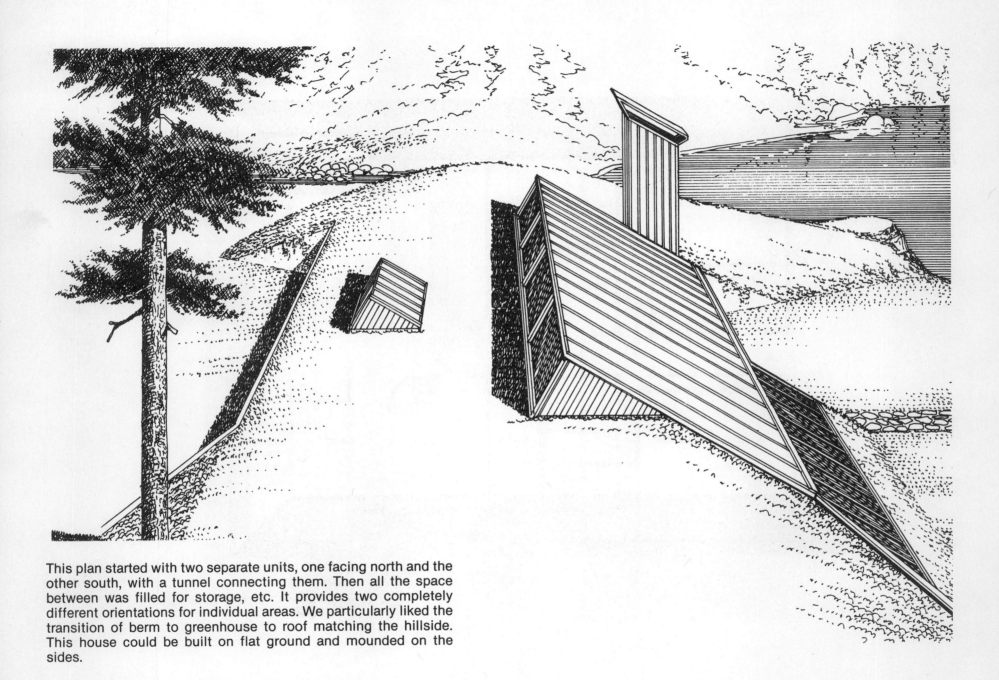

This plan started with two separate units, one facing north and the other south, with a tunnel connecting them. Then all the space between was filled for storage, etc. It provides two completely different orientations for individual areas. We particularly liked the transition of berm to greenhouse to roof matching the hillside. This house could be built on flat ground and mounded on the sides.

TWO-WAY PLAN — 1,960 S.F.

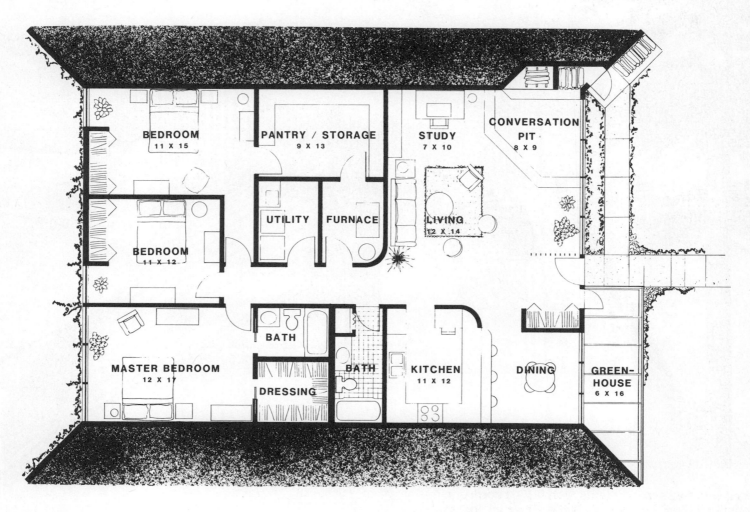

BEDROOM
11 X 15

PANTRY / STORAGE
9 X 13

STUDY
7 X 10

CONVERSATION
PIT
8 X 9

BEDROOM
11 X 12

UTILITY   FURNACE

LIVING
12 X 14

BATH

MASTER BEDROOM
12 X 17

DRESSING

BATH

KITCHEN
11 X 12

DINING

GREEN-
HOUSE
6 X 16

0   4   8

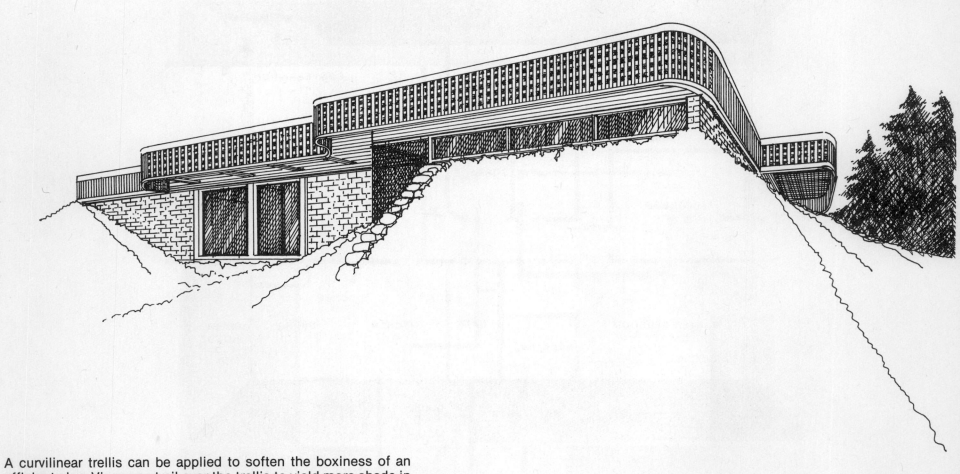

A curvilinear trellis can be applied to soften the boxiness of an efficient plan. Vines can trail over the trellis to yield more shade in the summer. High glass in the living room admits light only during the winter. With minor change to the plan, the entry could be moved next to the garage, and a window added to the kitchen. In this way, the entire east and west sides could be bermed.

EAST ENTRY — 1,420 S.F.

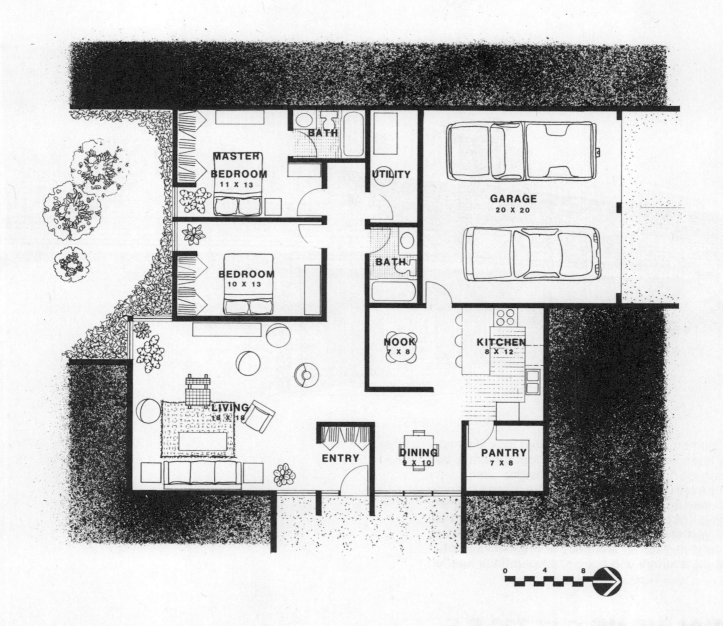

MASTER
BEDROOM
11 X 13

BATH

UTILITY

GARAGE
20 X 20

BEDROOM
10 X 13

BATH

LIVING
18 X 18

NOOK
7 X 8

KITCHEN
8 X 12

ENTRY

DINING
9 X 10

PANTRY
7 X 8

0 4 8

If you removed the berming from this home it would look like many other brick homes seen today. This serves to demonstrate two possibilities. (1) Perhaps some earth home designs aren't very different from what we are used to. (2) It is possible to modify some existing homes and take advantage of earth-sheltering. Both ideas are worth considering if you would like to reduce your heating bill by 25% to 80%. If you are considering modifying your existing home, be sure to consult with an architect or engineer to determine the structural capabilities and special preparations needed for exterior walls.

TRADITIONAL HOME — 1,730 S.F.

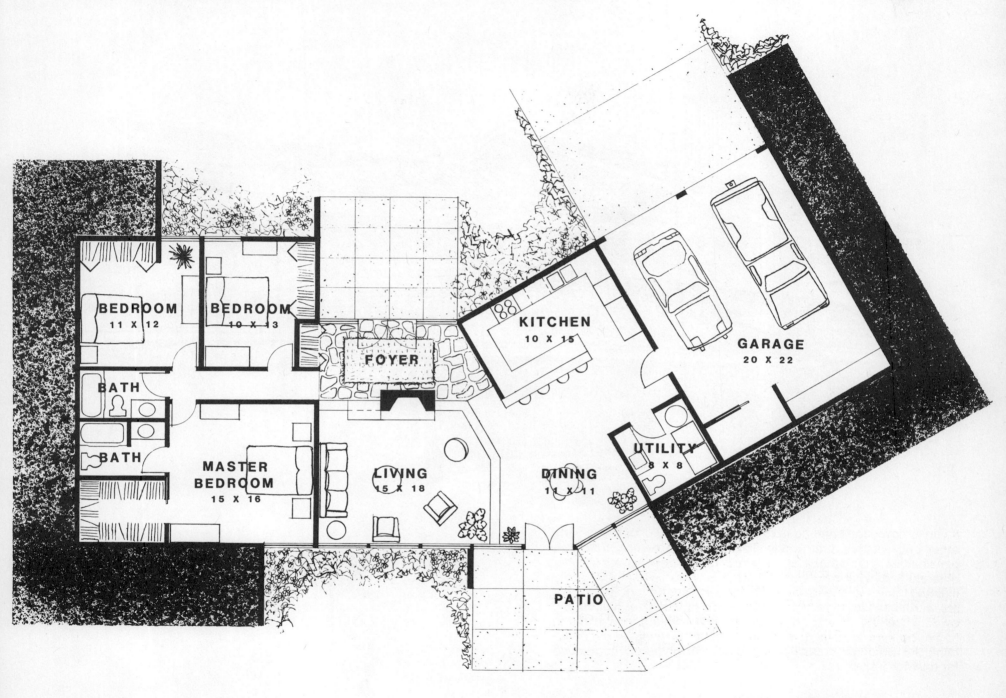

BEDROOM
11 X 12

BEDROOM
10 X 13

FOYER

KITCHEN
10 X 15

GARAGE
20 X 22

BATH

BATH

MASTER
BEDROOM
15 X 16

LIVING
15 X 18

DINING
11 X 11

UTILITY
8 X 8

PATIO

0 4 8

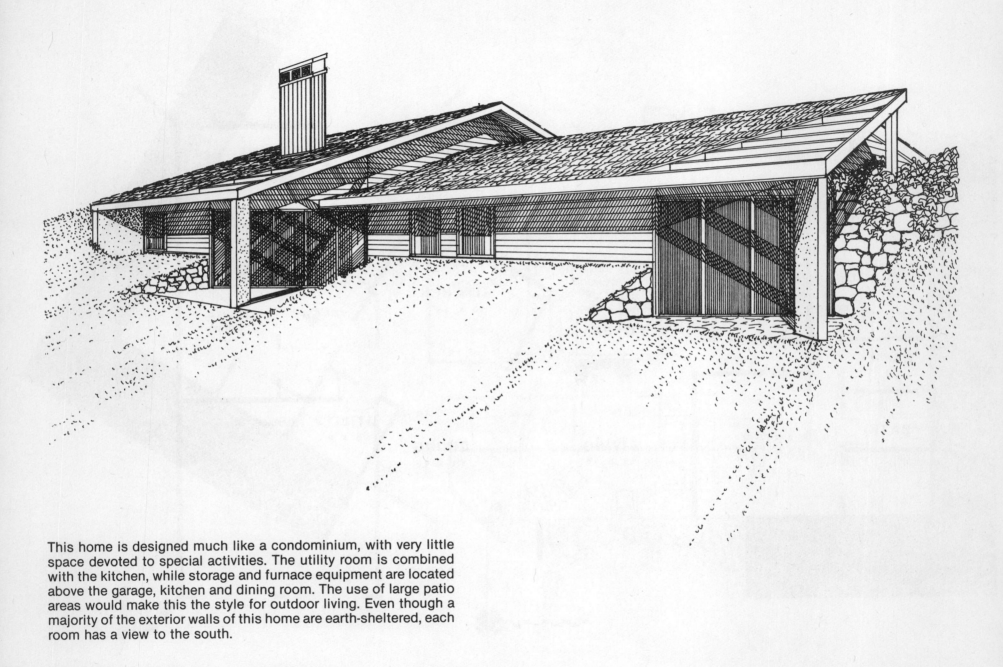

This home is designed much like a condominium, with very little space devoted to special activities. The utility room is combined with the kitchen, while storage and furnace equipment are located above the garage, kitchen and dining room. The use of large patio areas would make this the style for outdoor living. Even though a majority of the exterior walls of this home are earth-sheltered, each room has a view to the south.

PATIO HOME — 1,570 S.F.

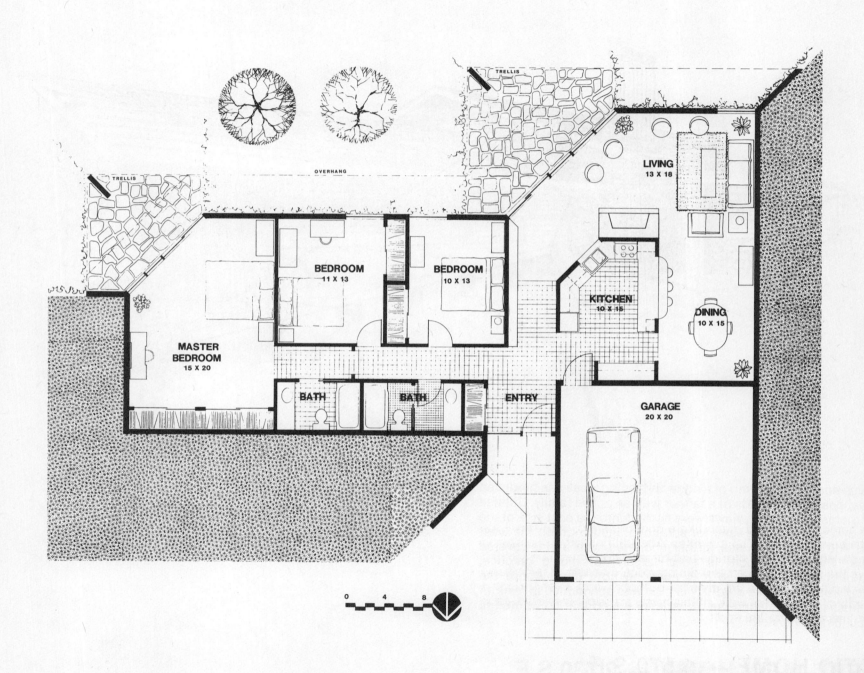

TRELLIS

TRELLIS

OVERHANG

LIVING
13 X 18

BEDROOM
11 X 13

BEDROOM
10 X 13

KITCHEN
10 X 15

DINING
10 X 15

MASTER
BEDROOM
15 X 20

BATH

BATH

ENTRY

GARAGE
20 X 20

0   4   8

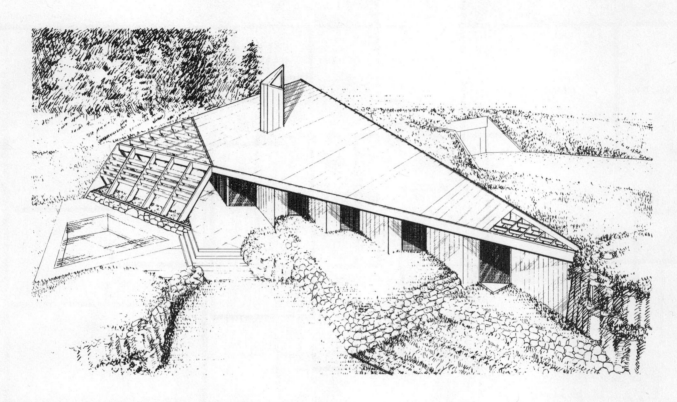

A large home near the top of a ridge and facing west was produced in response to the needs of a farmer with an active family. Utilities and rooms not needing views were backed into the east side of the plan and closets were used for additional insulation on the west side. The living room was further sheltered with a vine-covered trellis. The family room is used largely for music practice, recording, and lessons so it is near the front door. Above the dining area is a private study. This plan was abandoned in favor of the truss-roof plan when the owner announced that he wanted to try building it himself!

WEST-VIEW HOME — 2,730 S.F.

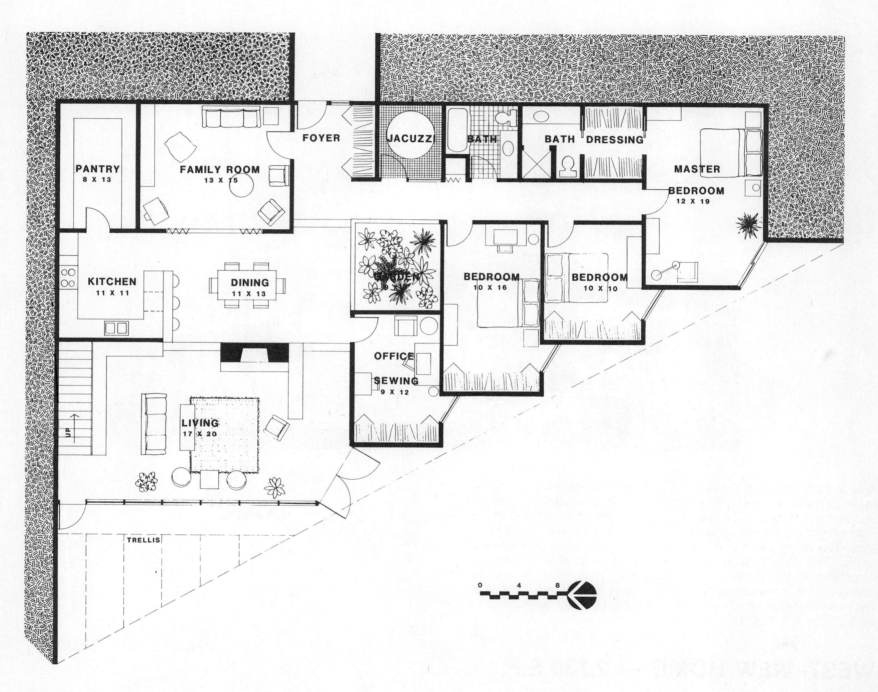

PANTRY
8 X 13

FAMILY ROOM
13 X 15

FOYER

JACUZZI

BATH

BATH

DRESSING

MASTER
BEDROOM
12 X 19

KITCHEN
11 X 11

DINING
11 X 13

GARDEN

BEDROOM
10 X 16

BEDROOM
10 X 10

OFFICE

SEWING
9 X 12

UP

LIVING
17 X 20

TRELLIS

0   4   8

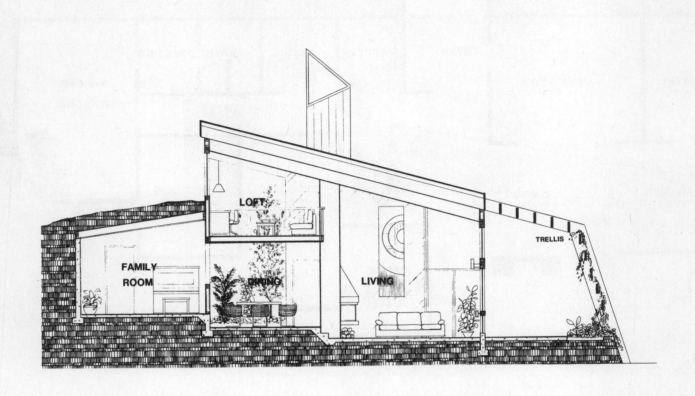

LOFT

FAMILY ROOM

DINING

LIVING

TRELLIS

0   4   8

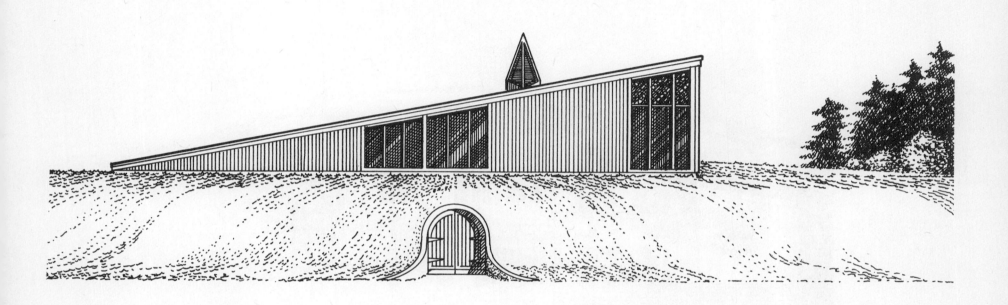

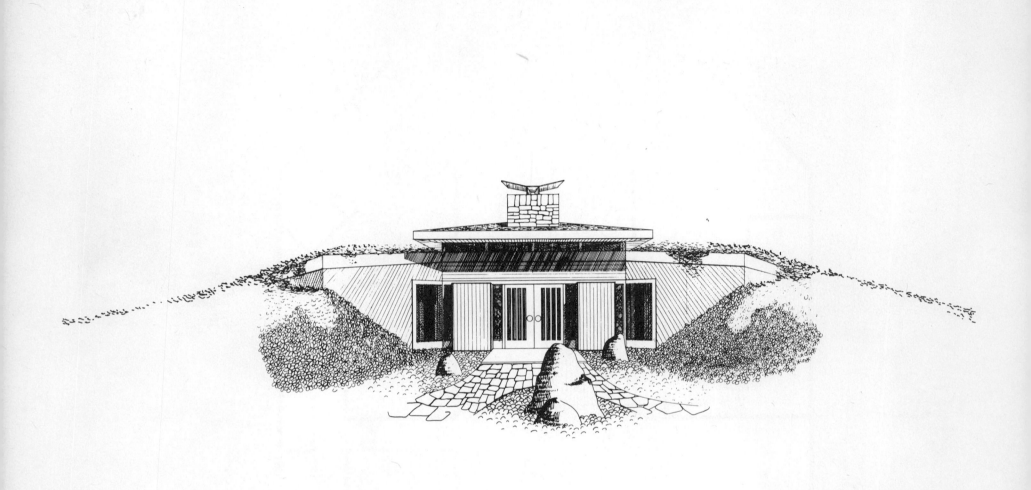

Developers questioned the concept of placing an "underground" home in a standard development so we showed them this plan. It brings two earth-covered wings up to shelter a central pavilion-style living area. The southern exposure looks on to a yard, patio, or pool. The developers finally agreed that no resident should complain because he couldn't see his neighbor. A garage could be attached at the family room.

TWO-WING HOME — 2,000 S.F.

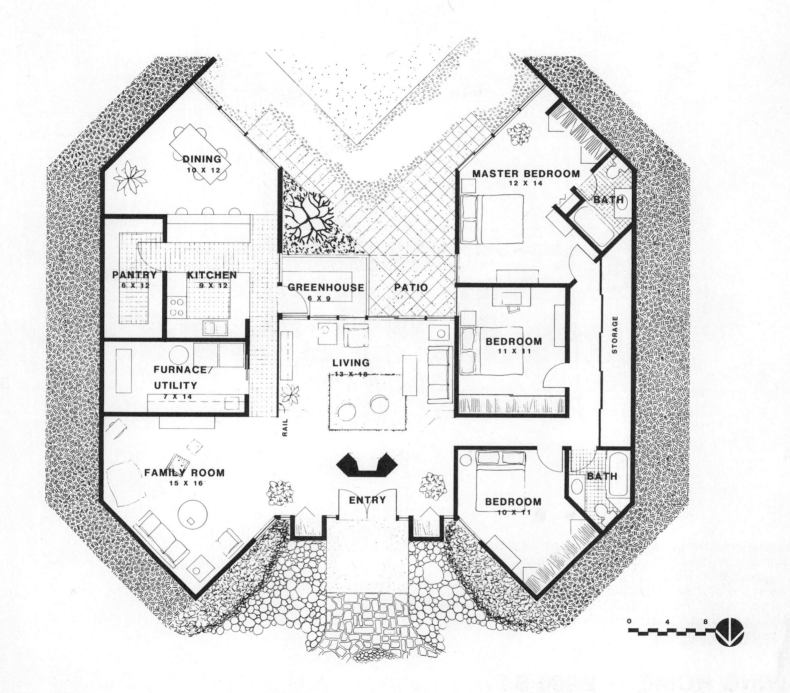

DINING
10 X 12

MASTER BEDROOM
12 X 14

BATH

PANTRY
6 X 12

KITCHEN
9 X 12

GREENHOUSE
6 X 9

PATIO

STORAGE

BEDROOM
11 X 11

FURNACE/
UTILITY
7 X 14

LIVING
13 X 48

RAIL

FAMILY ROOM
15 X 16

BEDROOM
10 X 11

BATH

ENTRY

0   4   8

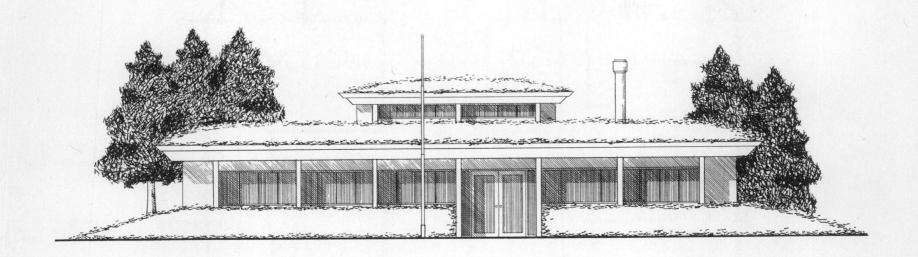

In southern climates where heat loss is not so severe, much can be done with overhangs. Berms are brought up to the window sill to shelter the lower wall and diminish reflected heat. Soil on the roof reduces daily temperature variations. Double glazing and insulating curtains would make this home quite comfortable in mild climates. It would be particularly nice in a heavily wooded area where trees provide much of the protection.

PAVILION HOME — 1,700 S.F.

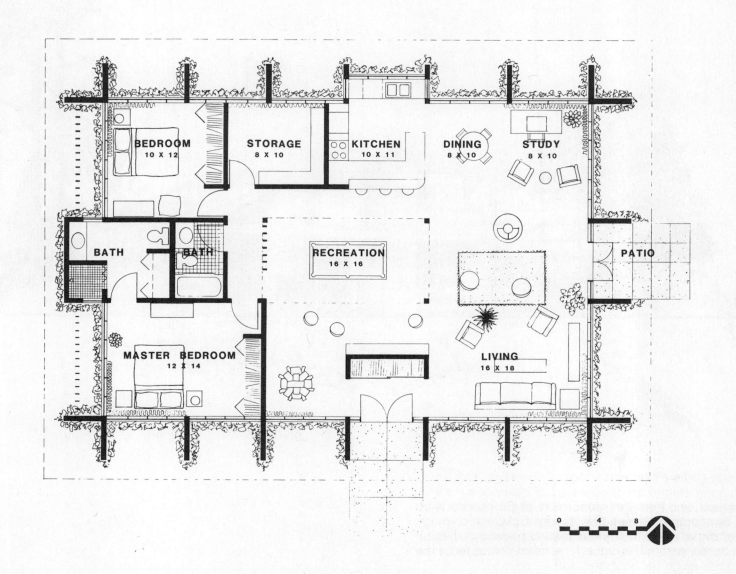

BEDROOM
10 X 12

STORAGE
8 X 10

KITCHEN
10 X 11

DINING
8 X 10

STUDY
8 X 10

BATH

BATH

RECREATION
16 X 16

PATIO

MASTER BEDROOM
12 X 14

LIVING
16 X 18

0   4   8

The Three-Bedroom and Four-Bedroom (next page) homes were designed for a development. The site was very rocky, which made it impractical to "dig in". The choice was made to develop a design concept which conformed to the natural free-form character of the area. (cont.)

THREE-BEDROOM HOME — 1,880 S.F.

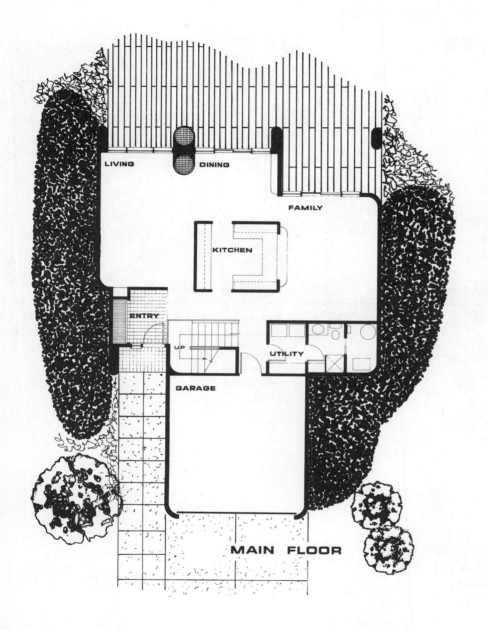

LIVING

DINING

FAMILY

KITCHEN

ENTRY

UP

UTILITY

GARAGE

MAIN FLOOR

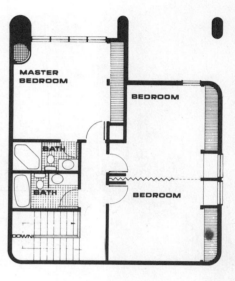

MASTER
BEDROOM

BEDROOM

BATH

BATH

BEDROOM

DOWN

UPPER FLOOR

We decided to use rocks to stabilize the berming and blend with existing site conditions. The berming also reduces the profile of two-story homes and enhances integration of site and structure. As seen from the illustration, the site is located at the top of a hill and exposed to all of the elements — a good reason for earth-sheltering. Some features of the homes include moving partitions between the childrens' bedrooms to allow for a larger play area in the winter, and kitchens accessible to both dining and family areas.

FOUR-BEDROOM HOME — 2,200 S.F.

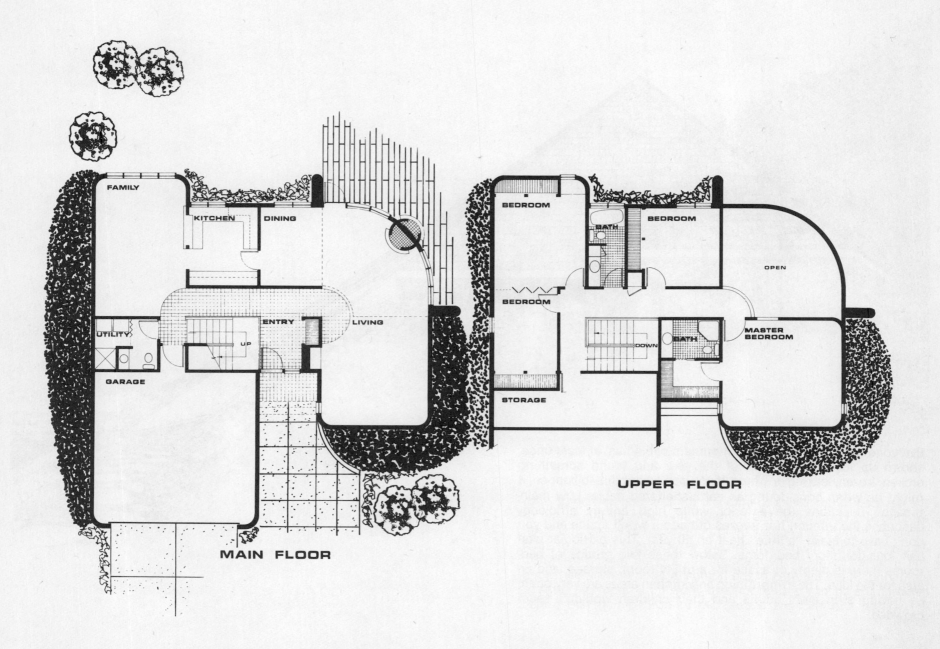

FAMILY

KITCHEN   DINING

UTILITY

ENTRY   LIVING

UP

GARAGE

MAIN FLOOR

BEDROOM

BATH   BEDROOM

OPEN

BEDROOM

DOWN   BATH   MASTER
BEDROOM

STORAGE

UPPER FLOOR

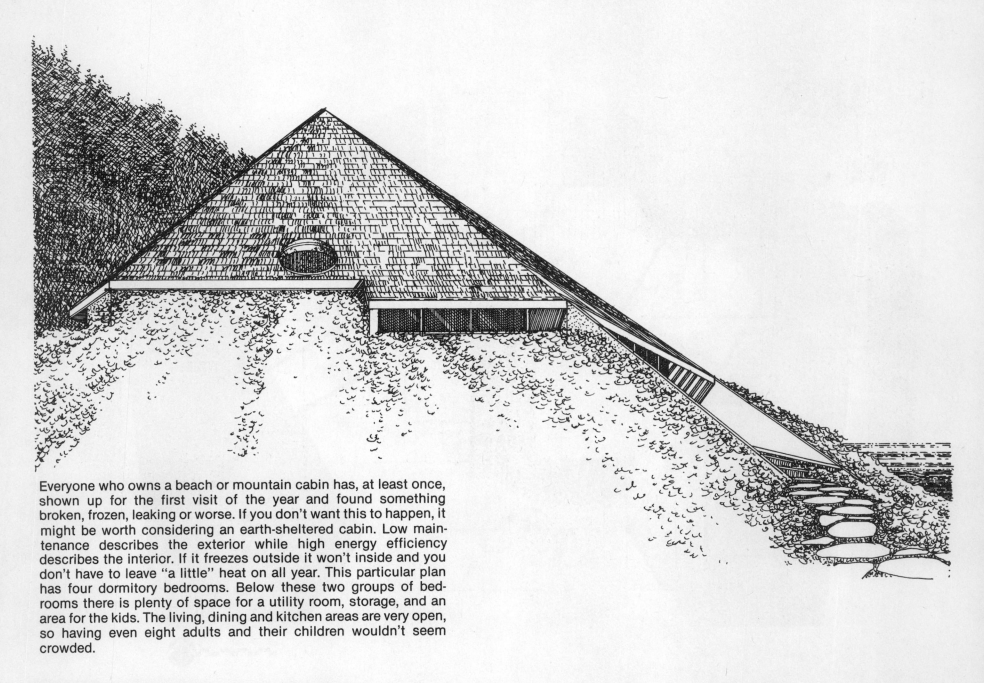

Everyone who owns a beach or mountain cabin has, at least once, shown up for the first visit of the year and found something broken, frozen, leaking or worse. If you don't want this to happen, it might be worth considering an earth-sheltered cabin. Low maintenance describes the exterior while high energy efficiency describes the interior. If it freezes outside it won't inside and you don't have to leave "a little" heat on all year. This particular plan has four dormitory bedrooms. Below these two groups of bedrooms there is plenty of space for a utility room, storage, and an area for the kids. The living, dining and kitchen areas are very open, so having even eight adults and their children wouldn't seem crowded.

BEACH CABIN — 2,150 S.F.

66

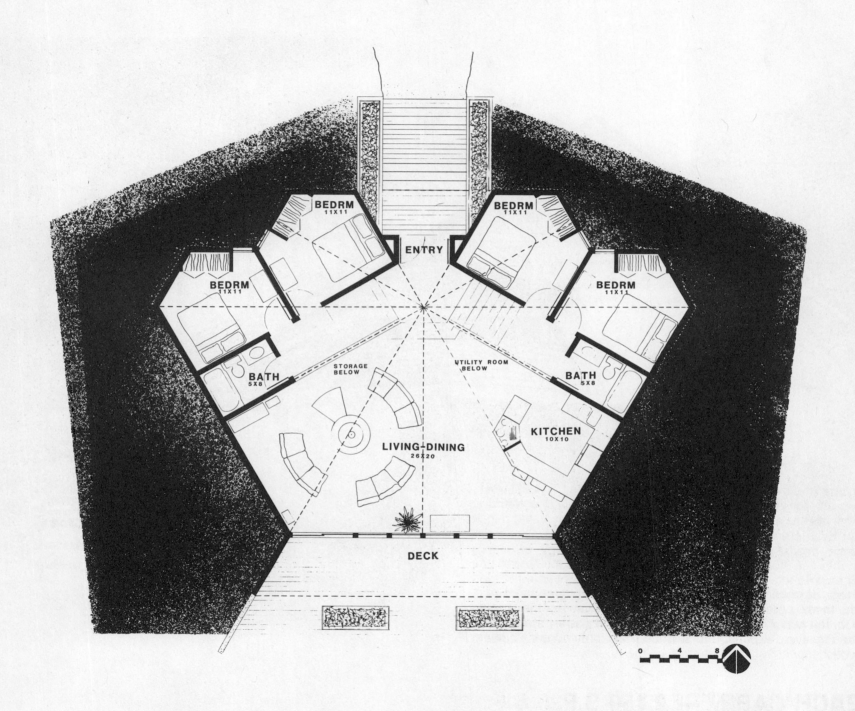

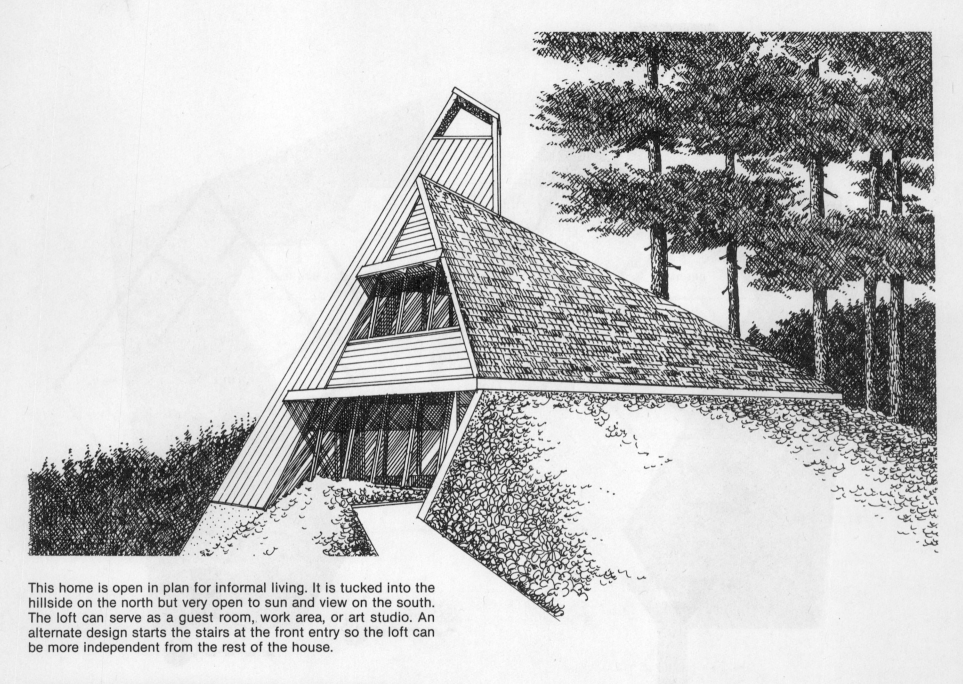

This home is open in plan for informal living. It is tucked into the hillside on the north but very open to sun and view on the south. The loft can serve as a guest room, work area, or art studio. An alternate design starts the stairs at the front entry so the loft can be more independent from the rest of the house.

MOUNTAIN RETREAT — 1,920 S.F.

68

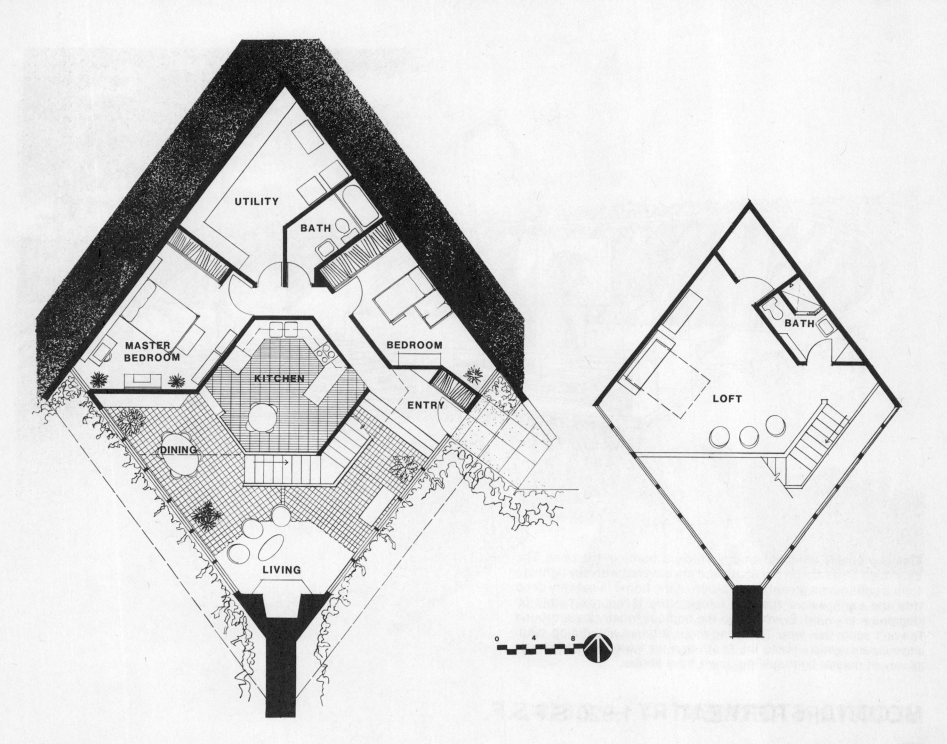

UTILITY

BATH

MASTER
BEDROOM

KITCHEN

BEDROOM

ENTRY

DINING

LIVING

LOFT

BATH

0   4   8

This is probably the most energy efficient home in the book. The only open areas are on the south and are covered with sky lights to form a continuous greenhouse. Much of the home is set very deep into the earth where the soil temperature is approximately 50 degrees year round. Even though the home is mostly underground it won't seem that way. The living-room, kitchen and dining room have a panoramic view to the south and the lower rooms will get plenty of natural light spilling down from above.

SECOND-STORY ENTRY — 2,540 S.F.

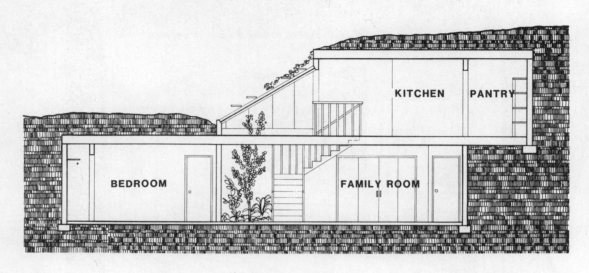

BEDROOM

KITCHEN PANTRY

FAMILY ROOM

SECTION

0   4   8

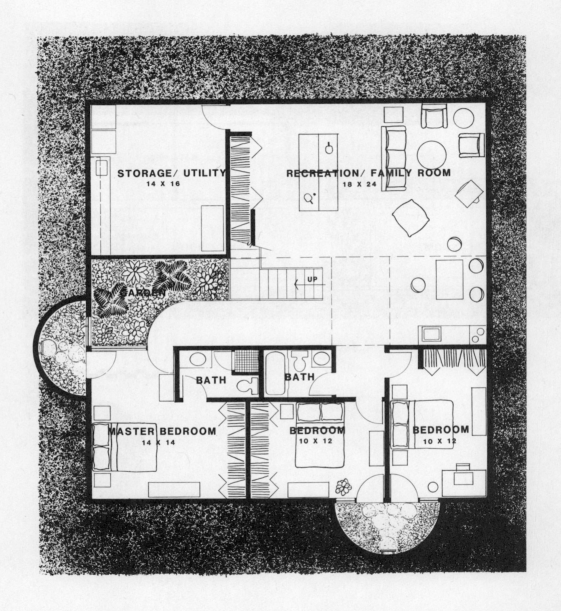

STORAGE/ UTILITY
14 X 16

RECREATION/ FAMILY ROOM
18 X 24

GARDEN

UP

BATH

BATH

MASTER BEDROOM
14 X 14

BEDROOM
10 X 12

BEDROOM
10 X 12

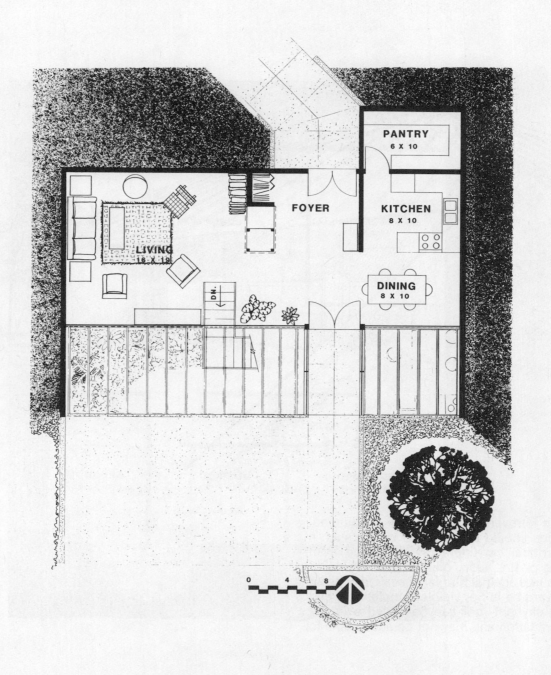

PANTRY
6 X 10

FOYER

KITCHEN
8 X 10

LIVING
16 X 19

DN.

DINING
8 X 10

0   4   8

Where there is no view, an introverted plan can be considered. Local interpretation of codes should be reviewed before such a design is finalized. The critical consideration is escape from "habitable" spaces in case of fire. Also, courtyard-facing doors and windows should be secured against burglary because once an intruder drops into a courtyard he is not visible to neighbors and can work uninterrupted. A skylight roof can be added over the atrium, but this reduces ventilation and may not be acceptable to building officials.

ATRIUM HOME — 2,770 S.F.

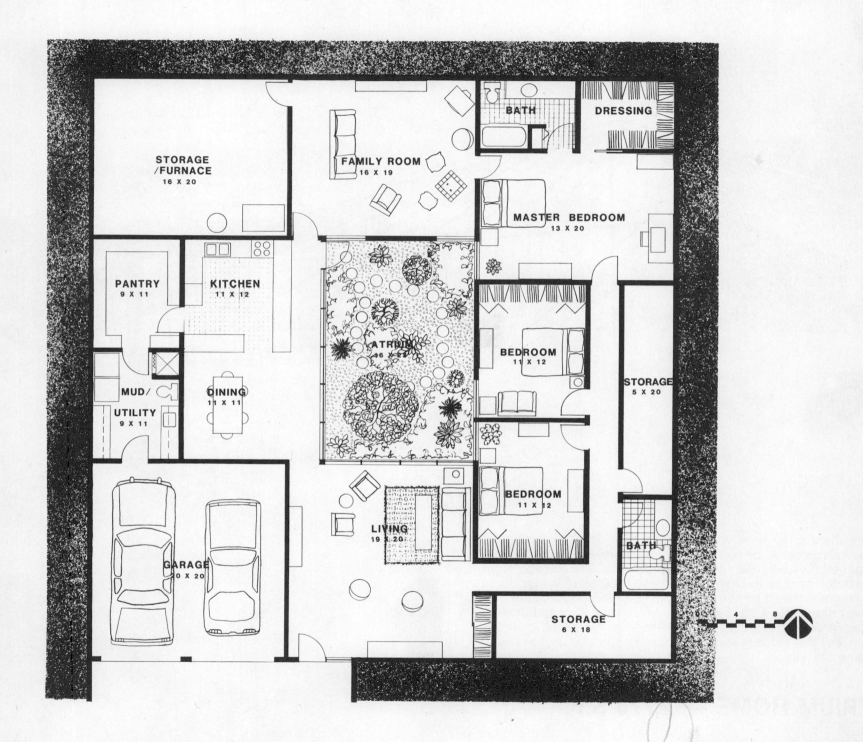

STORAGE
/FURNACE
16 X 20

FAMILY ROOM
16 X 19

BATH

DRESSING

MASTER BEDROOM
13 X 20

PANTRY
9 X 11

KITCHEN
11 X 12

ATRIUM
26 X 28

BEDROOM
11 X 12

STORAGE
5 X 20

MUD/
UTILITY
9 X 11

DINING
11 X 11

BEDROOM
11 X 12

GARAGE
20 X 20

LIVING
19 X 20

BATH

STORAGE
6 X 18

0   4   8

75

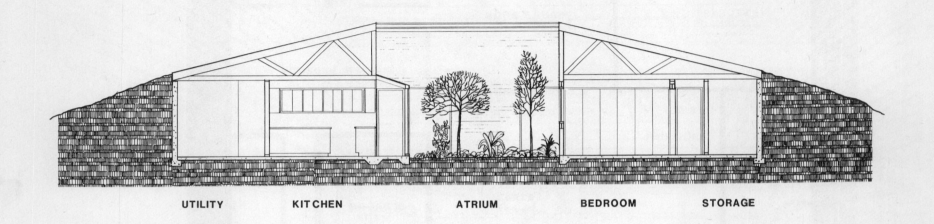

UTILITY   KITCHEN   ATRIUM   BEDROOM   STORAGE

0   4   8

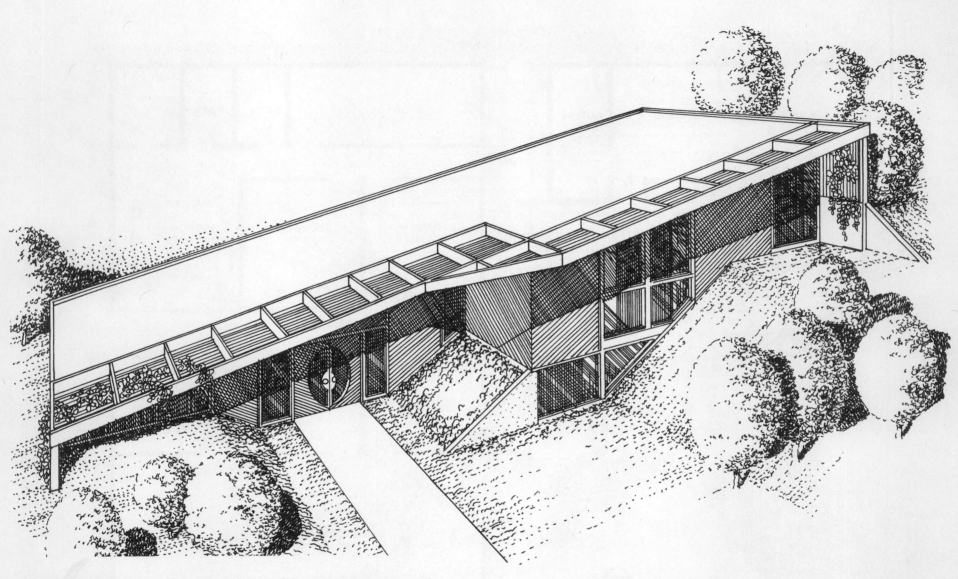

A popular builder home style uses three levels for efficiency of construction without more than a half level drop between floors. Keeping living areas to the south side makes this a reasonable arrangement, particularly for east or west slopes.

SPLIT-LEVEL HOME — 2,750 S.F.

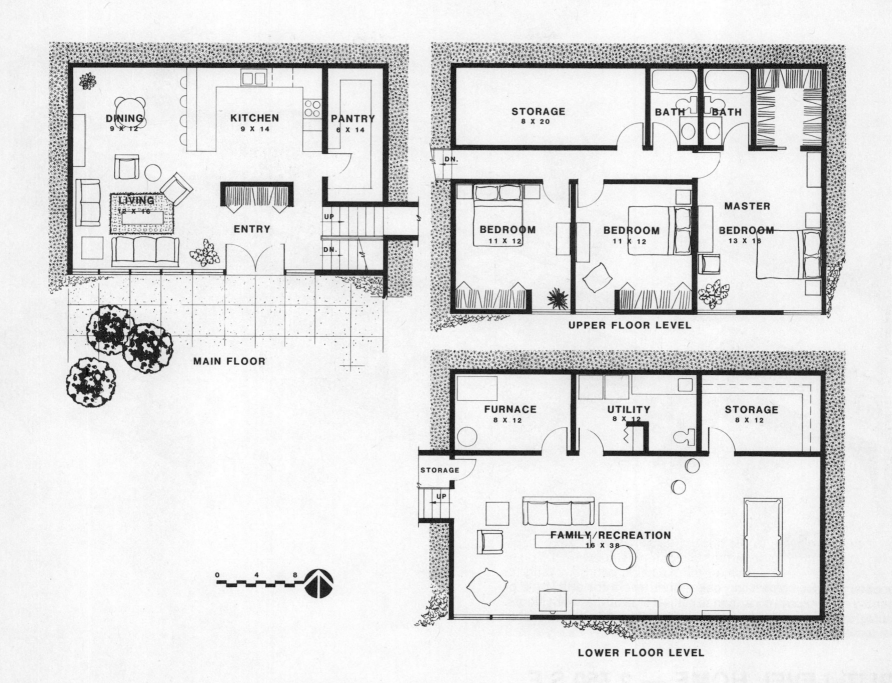

DINING
9 X 12

KITCHEN
9 X 14

PANTRY
6 X 14

LIVING
12 X 16

ENTRY

UP

DN.

MAIN FLOOR

0   4   8

STORAGE
8 X 20

BATH

BATH

DN.

BEDROOM
11 X 12

BEDROOM
11 X 12

MASTER

BEDROOM
13 X 16

UPPER FLOOR LEVEL

FURNACE
8 X 12

UTILITY
8 X 12

STORAGE
8 X 12

STORAGE

UP

FAMILY/RECREATION
16 X 38

LOWER FLOOR LEVEL

SPLIT-LEVEL HOME — 2,150 S.F.

When a desired view is to the north, it is still possible to collect passive solar energy through high clerestory windows. This plan can be even more efficient when the backside bedroom wing is wide enough for windows to peek around the front unit. In this way, more berming can be arranged on the sides. Notice that draft deflectors are used on hillside homes or wherever chimney tops are close to the ground.

NORTH-VIEW HOME — 1,650 S.F.

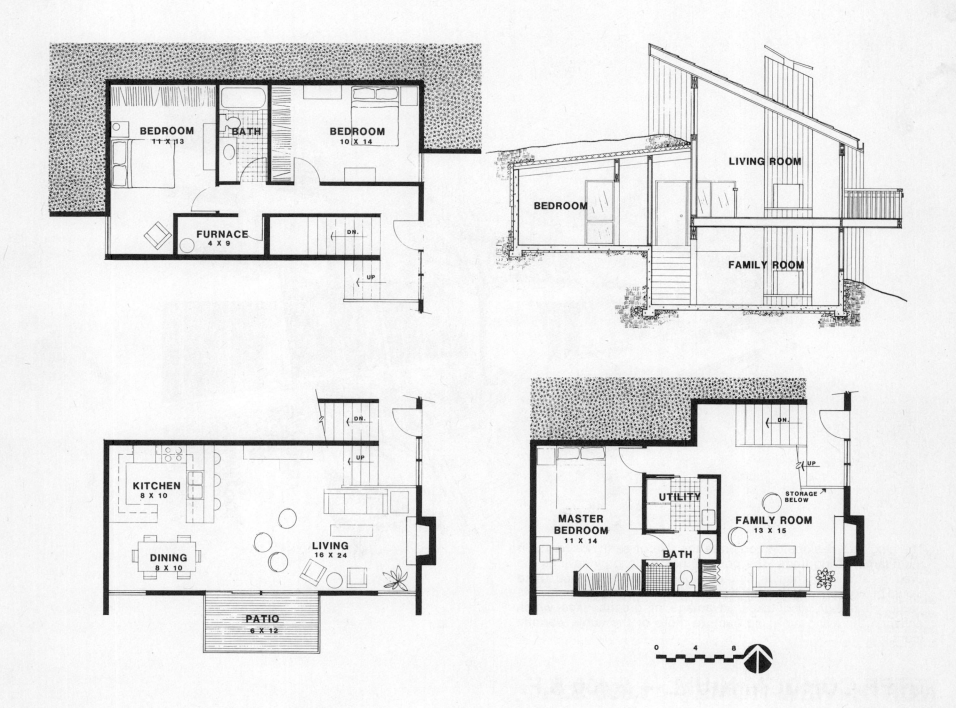

BEDROOM
11 X 13

BATH

BEDROOM
10 X 14

FURNACE
4 X 9

DN.

UP

LIVING ROOM

BEDROOM

FAMILY ROOM

KITCHEN
8 X 10

DN.

UP

LIVING
16 X 24

DINING
8 X 10

PATIO
6 X 12

DN.

UP

MASTER
BEDROOM
11 X 14

UTILITY

STORAGE
BELOW

FAMILY ROOM
13 X 15

BATH

0   4   8

The next four designs demonstrate the use of earth-sheltering in multi-family living units. The possibilities for energy savings are even greater here than in single-family residences, since there would be no heat loss through the common walls of each unit. This particular design also takes advantage of greenhouses which enhance the living area and capture more of the sun's warmth. (cont.)

STEP CONDOMINIUM — 2,400 S.F.

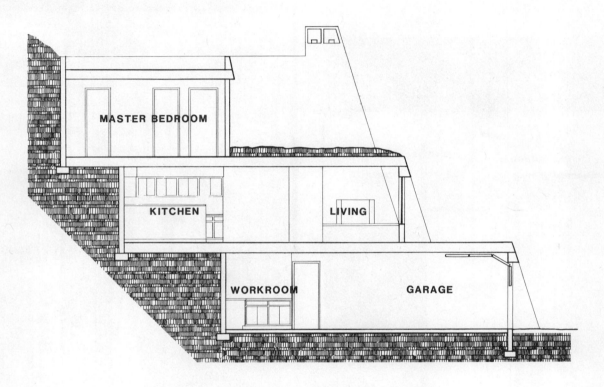

MASTER BEDROOM

KITCHEN

LIVING

WORKROOM

GARAGE

SECTION

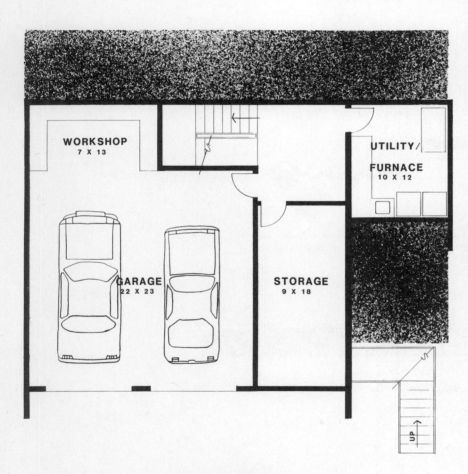

WORKSHOP
7 X 13

UTILITY/
FURNACE
10 X 12

GARAGE
22 X 23

STORAGE
9 X 18

UP

FIRST FLOOR PLAN

STUDY
10 X 13

FAMILY ROOM
10 X 16

KITCHEN
10 X 13

LIVING
13 X 18

GREENHOUSE

DINING
9 X 11

PATIO

DN.

SECOND FLOOR PLAN

0   4   8

84

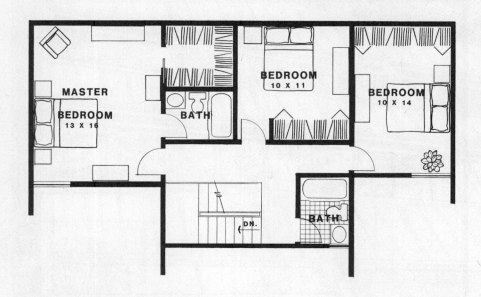

MASTER
BEDROOM
13 X 16

BATH

BEDROOM
10 X 11

BEDROOM
10 X 14

DN.

BATH

THIRD FLOOR PLAN

0   4   8

This style of construction would make it practical to build on very steep sites which could not be used otherwise. Each unit or room above would be stepped back to match the slope of the hill. (cont.)

SLOPE CONDOMINIUM — 1,800 S.F.

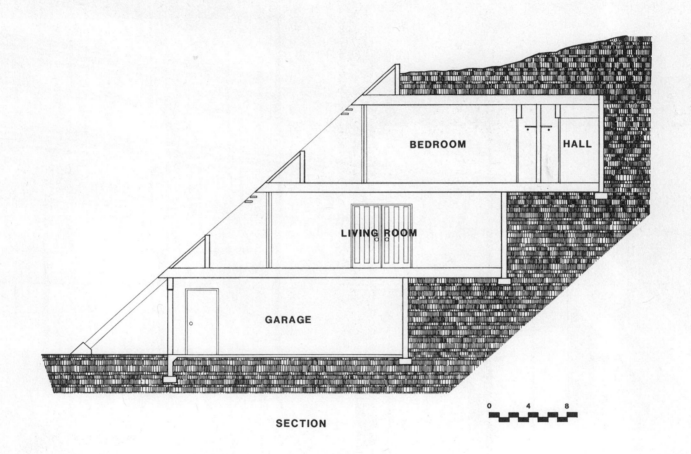

BEDROOM

HALL

LIVING ROOM

GARAGE

SECTION

0   4   8

87

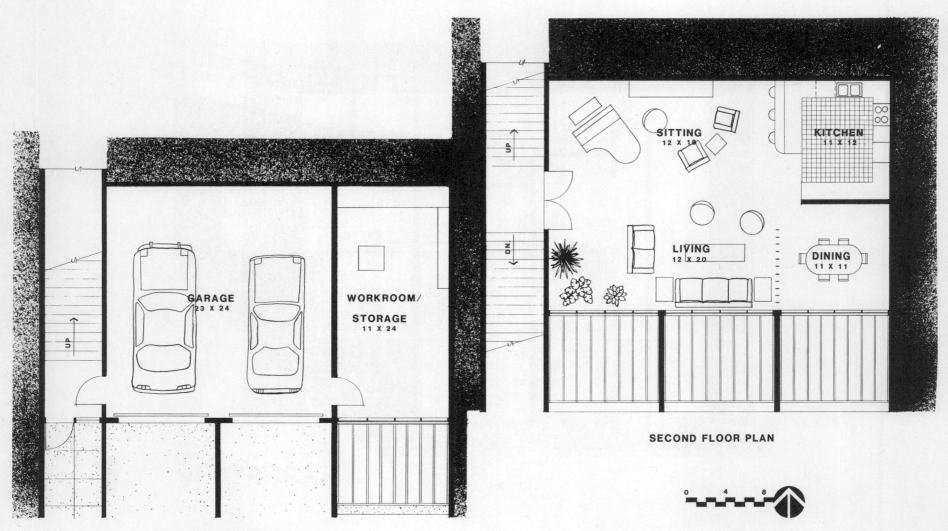

GARAGE
23 X 24

WORKROOM/ STORAGE
11 X 24

UP

DN.

UP

UP

SITTING
12 X 18

KITCHEN
11 X 12

LIVING
12 X 20

DINING
11 X 11

FIRST FLOOR PLAN

SECOND FLOOR PLAN

0   4   8

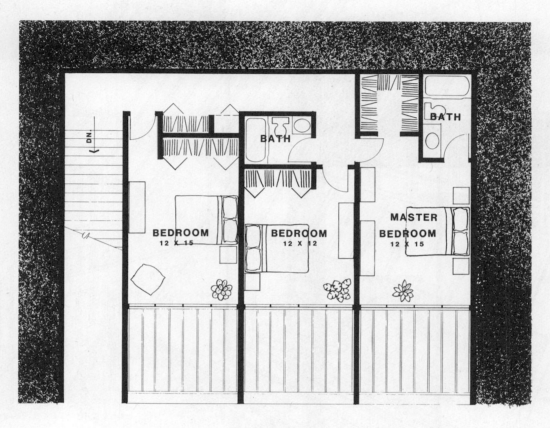

THIRD FLOOR PLAN

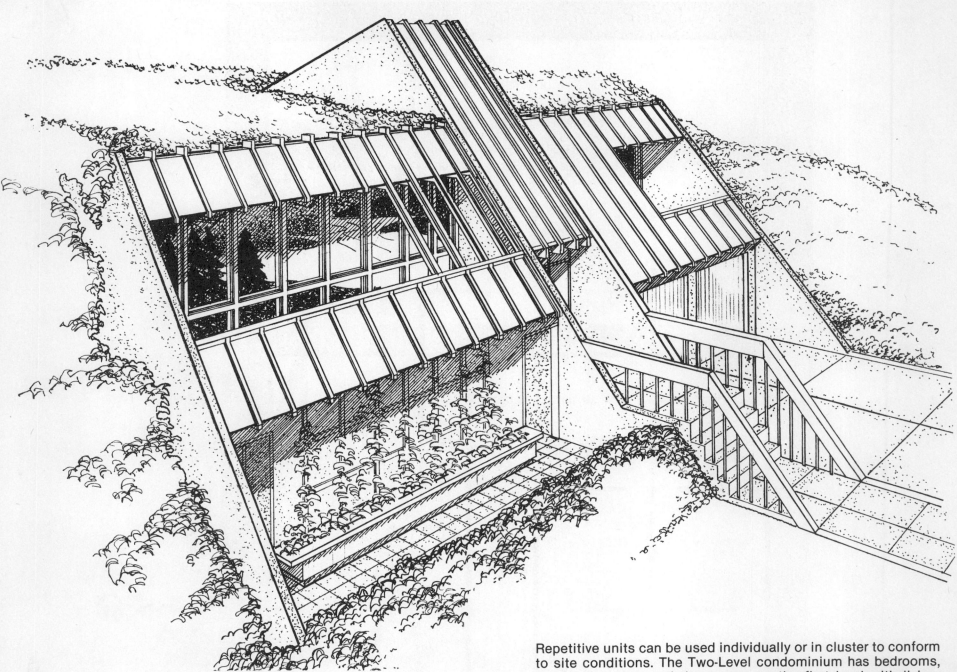

TWO-LEVEL CONDOMINIUM — 1,900 S.F.

Repetitive units can be used individually or in cluster to conform to site conditions. The Two-Level condominium has bedrooms, the family room, and the garage on the first level with living, dining and master bedroom above to take advantage of the view. (cont.)

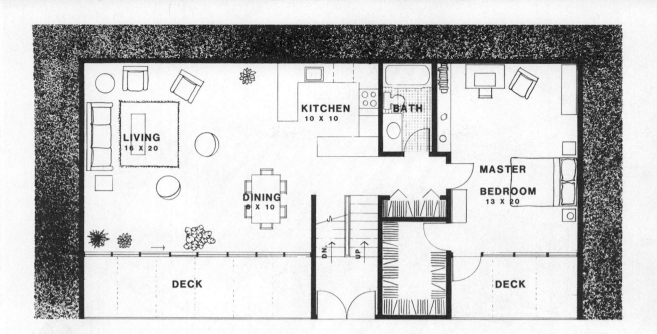

LIVING
16 X 20

KITCHEN
10 X 10

BATH

MASTER
BEDROOM
13 X 20

DINING
8 X 10

DN

UP

DECK

DECK

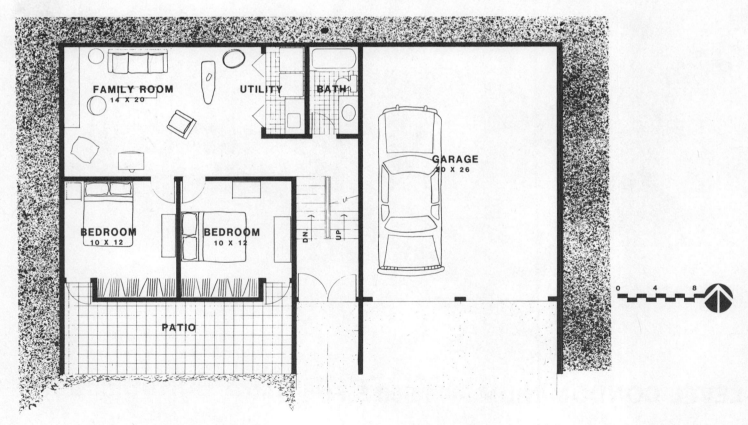

FAMILY ROOM
14 X 20

UTILITY

BATH

GARAGE
20 X 26

BEDROOM
10 X 12

BEDROOM
10 X 12

DN

UP

PATIO

0   4   8

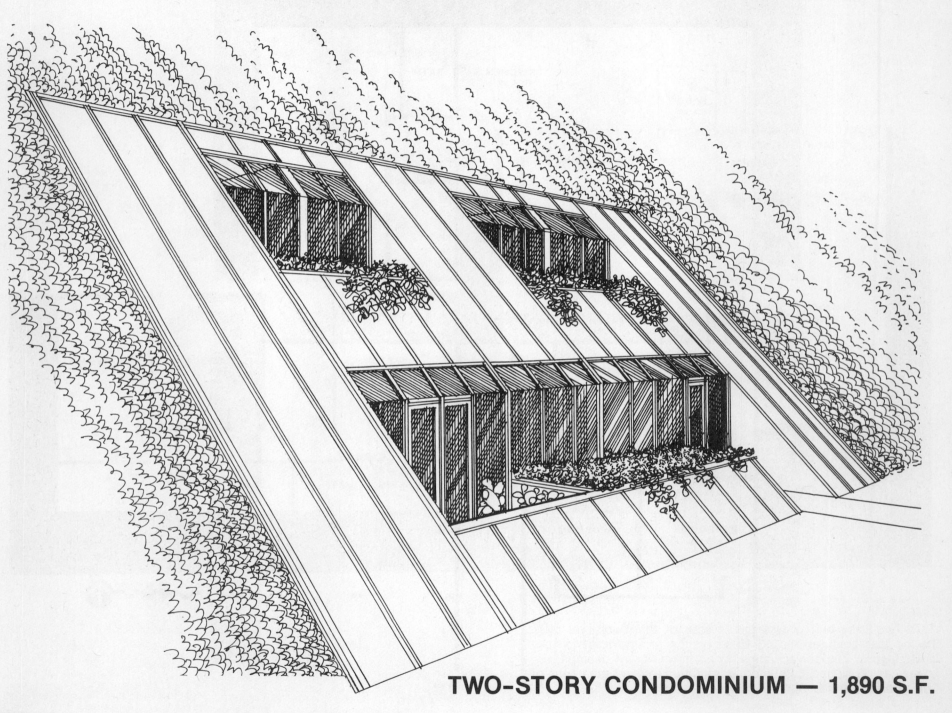

TWO-STORY CONDOMINIUM — 1,890 S.F.

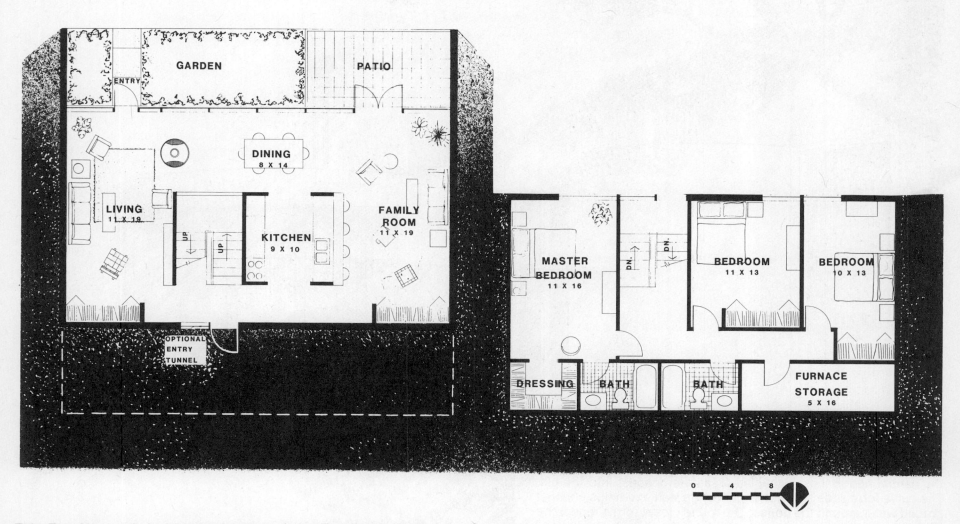

GARDEN

PATIO

ENTRY

DINING
8 X 14

LIVING
11 X 19

UP

UP

KITCHEN
9 X 10

FAMILY
ROOM
11 X 19

OPTIONAL
ENTRY
TUNNEL

MASTER
BEDROOM
11 X 16

DN.

DN.

BEDROOM
11 X 13

BEDROOM
10 X 13

DRESSING

BATH

BATH

FURNACE
STORAGE
5 X 16

0   4   8

This Two-Story unit is just the reverse of the Two-Level plan, having the family and living areas on the ground level to take advantage of outdoor activities. In all the different designs, the plans can be flipped, combined, or modified to meet the needs of the owners, the site, and the budget.

An exposed living area is projected in front of a sheltered support area to provide a snail-shaped plan which seems to wind around the central hearth. Less-occupied areas are deepest into the hill. The curve form adds some strength to the wall and helps channel ground water around the house. The round closet forms repeat the living room form and give an appearance of units attached to the hill.

SNAIL PLAN — 1,450 S.F.

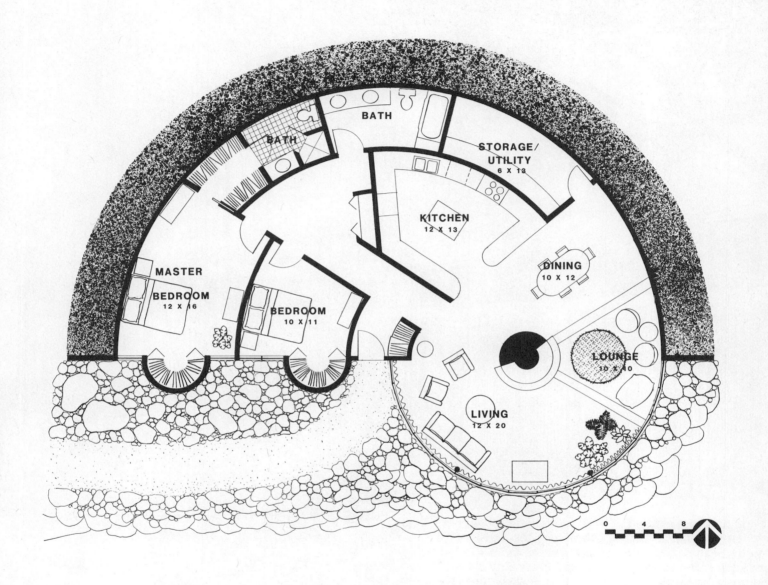

BATH

BATH

STORAGE/
UTILITY
6 X 13

KITCHEN
12 X 13

DINING
10 X 12

MASTER
BEDROOM
12 X 16

BEDROOM
10 X 11

LOUNGE
10 X 10

LIVING
12 X 20

0   4   8

The next three designs make use of circular formwork and concrete shapes used in the construction of grain elevators and water storage tanks. (cont.)

THREE-CURVE PLAN — 1,600 S.F.

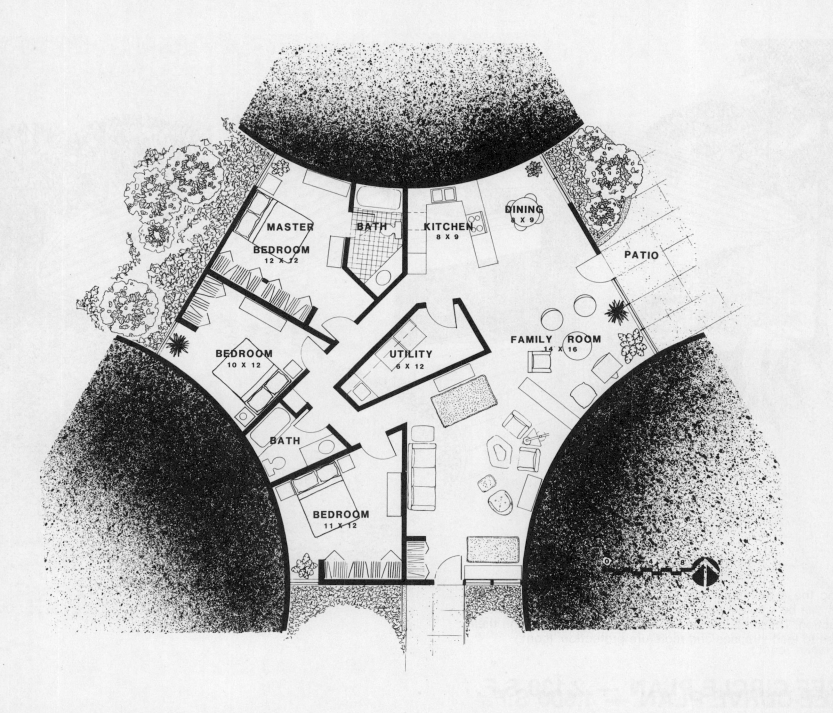

MASTER
BEDROOM
12 X 12

BATH

KITCHEN
8 X 9

DINING
8 X 9

PATIO

BEDROOM
10 X 12

UTILITY
6 X 12

FAMILY ROOM
14 X 16

BATH

BEDROOM
11 X 12

97

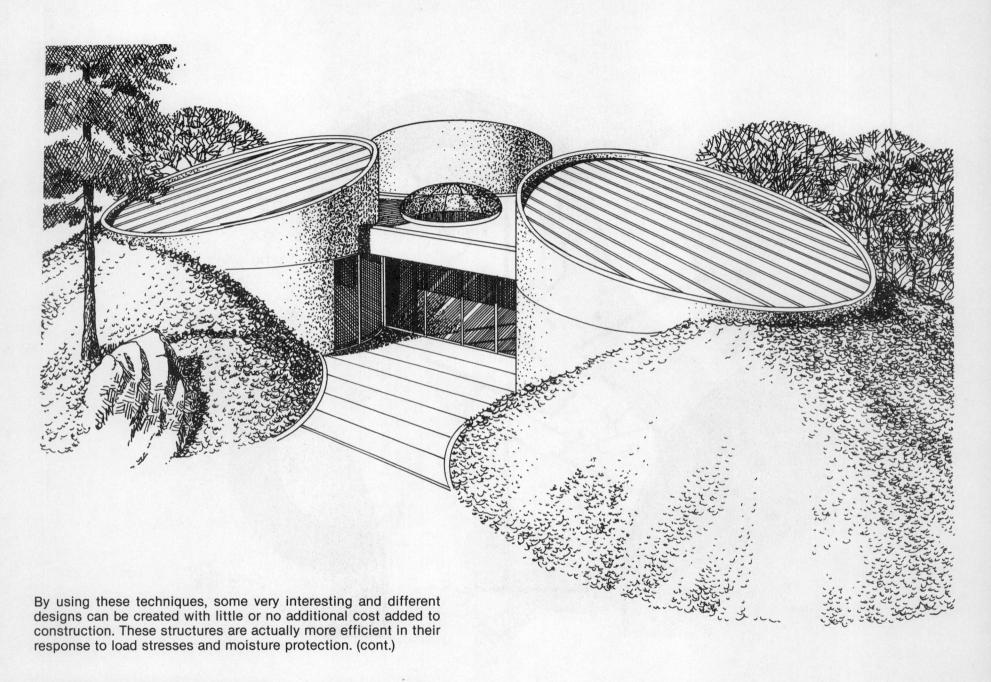

By using these techniques, some very interesting and different designs can be created with little or no additional cost added to construction. These structures are actually more efficient in their response to load stresses and moisture protection. (cont.)

THREE-CIRCLE PLAN — 2,130 S.F.

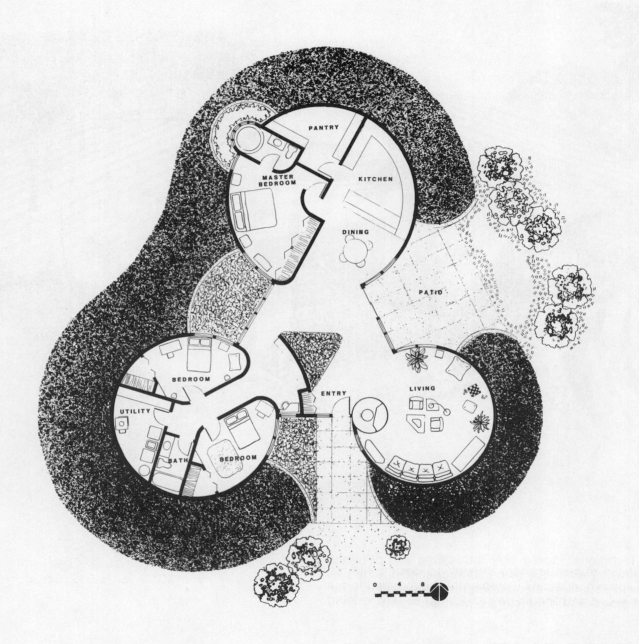

PANTRY

KITCHEN

MASTER
BEDROOM

DINING

PATIO

BEDROOM

UTILITY

ENTRY

LIVING

BATH

BEDROOM

0 4 8

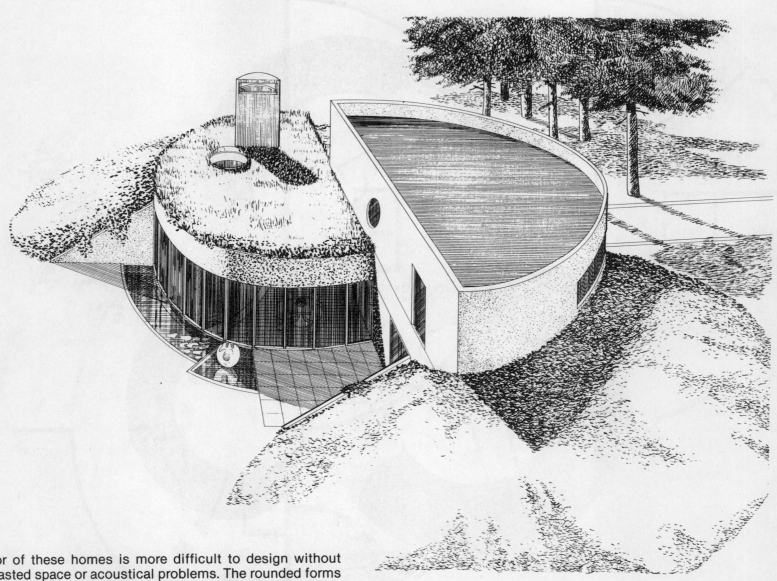

The interior of these homes is more difficult to design without creating wasted space or acoustical problems. The rounded forms reflect and focus sound and should be considered when choosing finish materials.

SEMI-CIRCLES PLAN — 2,500 S.F.

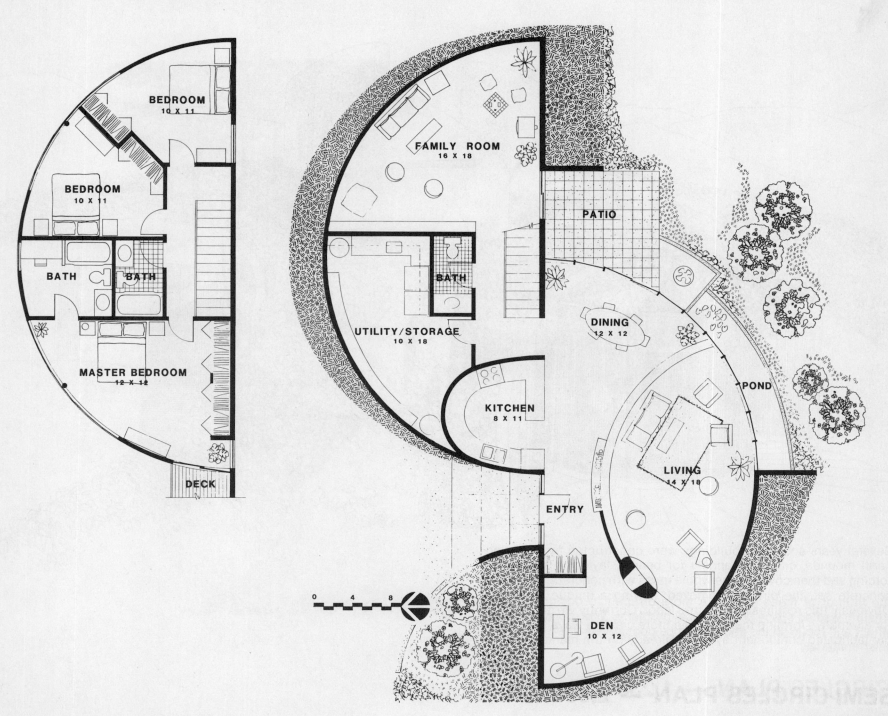

BEDROOM
10 X 11

BEDROOM
10 X 11

MASTER BEDROOM
12 X 12

BATH

BATH

DECK

FAMILY ROOM
16 X 18

PATIO

UTILITY/STORAGE
10 X 18

BATH

DINING
12 X 12

KITCHEN
8 X 11

POND

LIVING
14 X 18

ENTRY

DEN
10 X 12

0   4   8

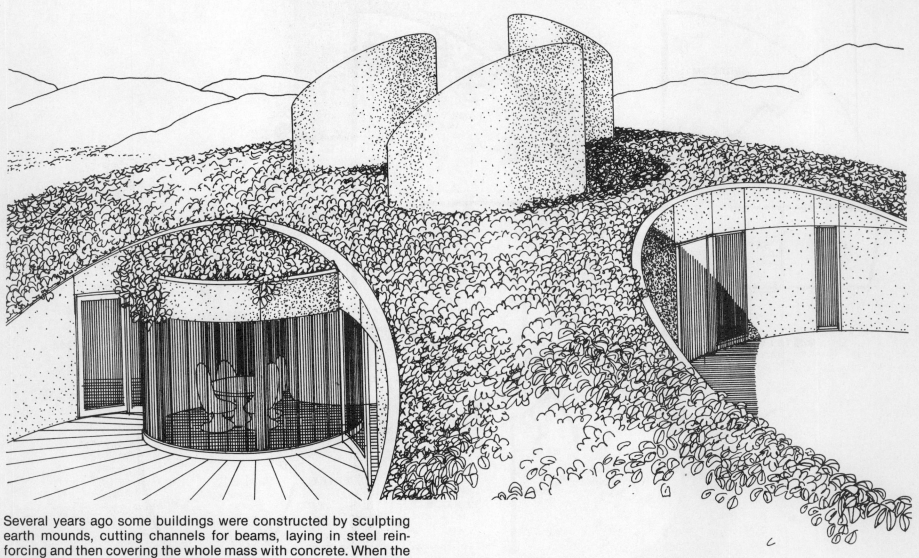

Several years ago some buildings were constructed by sculpting earth mounds, cutting channels for beams, laying in steel reinforcing and then covering the whole mass with concrete. When the concrete set, the dirt was removed, leaving a unique structure. Obviously this requires almost free labor. Currently we are looking for alternative forming methods and more creative ways to use the pre-fabricated component systems already on the market.

CIRCLES PLAN — 1,230 S.F.

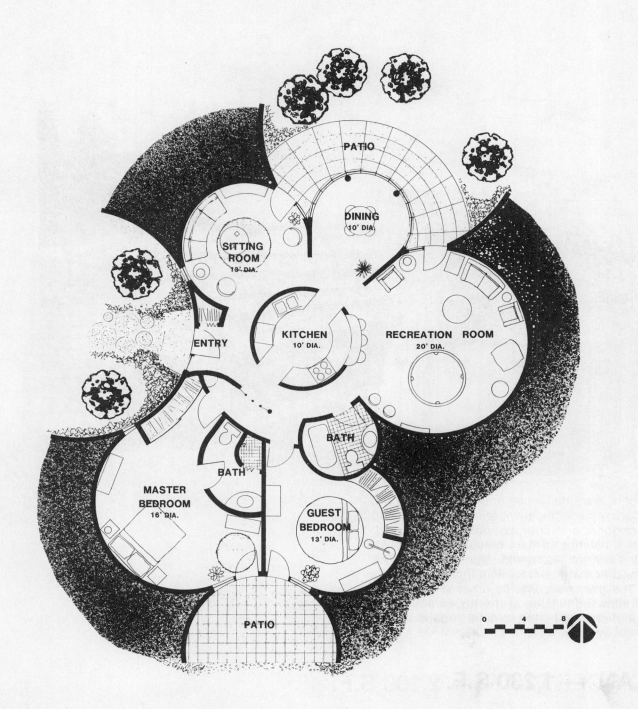

PATIO

DINING
10' DIA.

SITTING
ROOM
13' DIA.

ENTRY

KITCHEN
10' DIA.

RECREATION ROOM
20' DIA.

BATH

BATH

MASTER
BEDROOM
16' DIA.

GUEST
BEDROOM
13' DIA.

PATIO

0 — 4 — 8

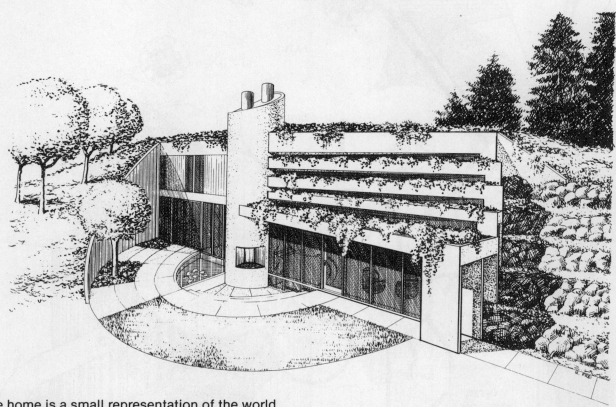

For some people, the home is a small representation of the world, where various elements are represented symbolically. Here the full circle is divided into exterior and interior, natural and controlled, land and water, to form a balance of harmonious elements. All members radiate from the central hearth and structural mast. The living room is covered by a floating terrace, with light penetrating between each planter. The planters come together at the house center but flair out to follow the hillside at the house perimeter. The shadow pattern would change by the minute throughout the day.

SYMBOLIC CIRCLE PLAN — 2,100 S.F.

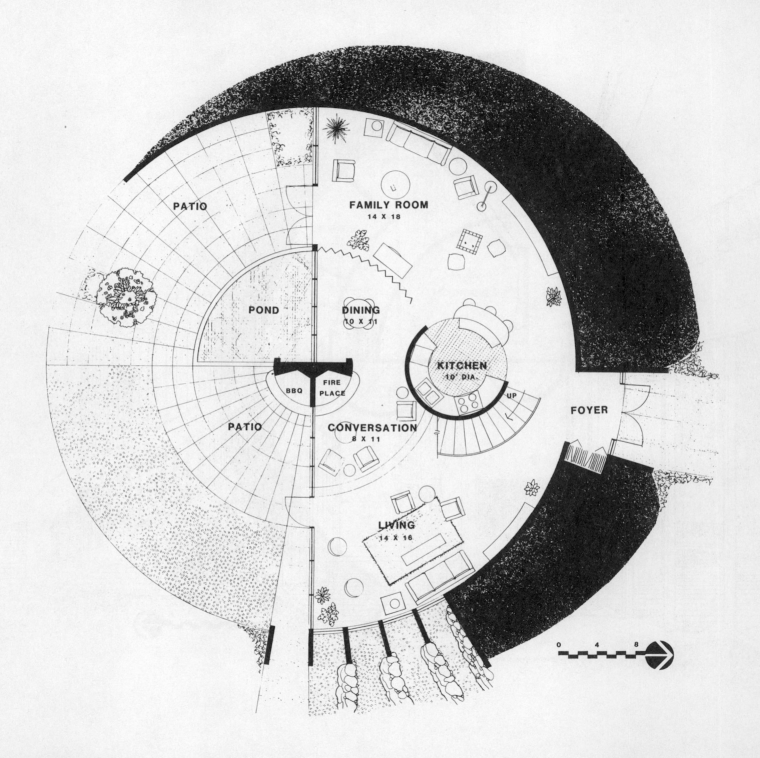

PATIO

FAMILY ROOM
14 X 18

POND

DINING
10 X 11

KITCHEN
10' DIA.

FOYER

BBQ

FIRE
PLACE

UP

PATIO

CONVERSATION
8 X 11

LIVING
14 X 16

0   4   8

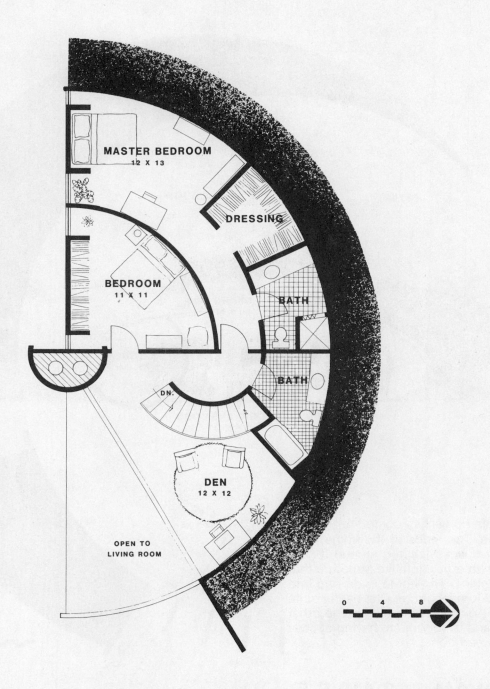

MASTER BEDROOM
12 X 13

DRESSING

BEDROOM
11 X 11

BATH

BATH

DN.

DEN
12 X 12

OPEN TO
LIVING ROOM

0   4   8

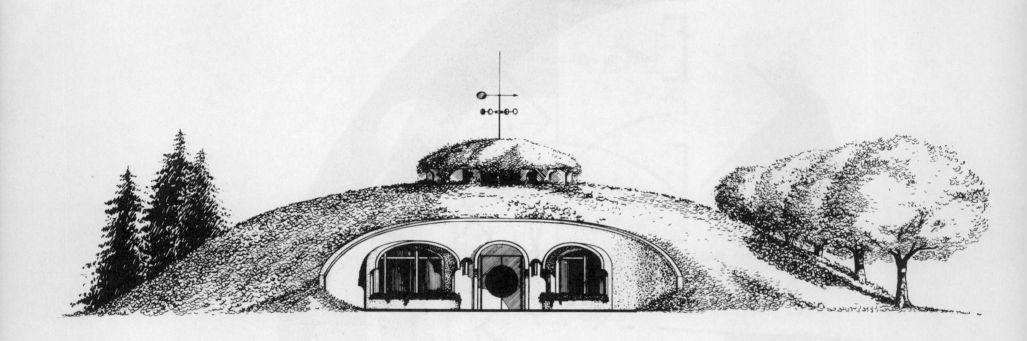

We like to think the design of this home has come "full circle" since it started out as a rectangle. The focus of the home is, of course, the atrium, with all other spaces located around it. The atrium is enclosed and covered with a pavilion-like structure that admits indirect sunlight from all sides. The home is divided into two hemispheres by the entry and furnace room. One half is quite enclosed and private, for sleeping or just being alone. The other side is used for family activities and is very open, having spaces defined only by furniture and one partition.

ATRIUM-MOUND PLAN — 3,410 S.F.

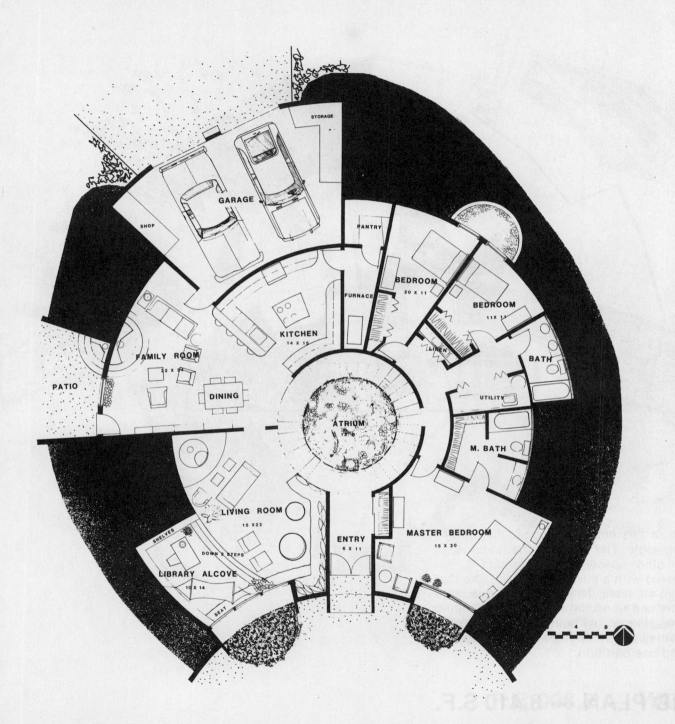

STORAGE

SHOP

GARAGE

PANTRY

BEDROOM
20 X 11

BEDROOM
11 X 11

KITCHEN
14 X 15

FURNACE

BATH

FAMILY ROOM
22 X 24

LINEN

PATIO

DINING

UTILITY

ATRIUM

M. BATH

LIVING ROOM
15 X 22

SHELVES

DOWN 2 STEPS

ENTRY
6 X 11

MASTER BEDROOM
15 X 20

LIBRARY ALCOVE
10 X 14

SEAT

ATRIUM HOUSE PLAN #C8A410 S.F.

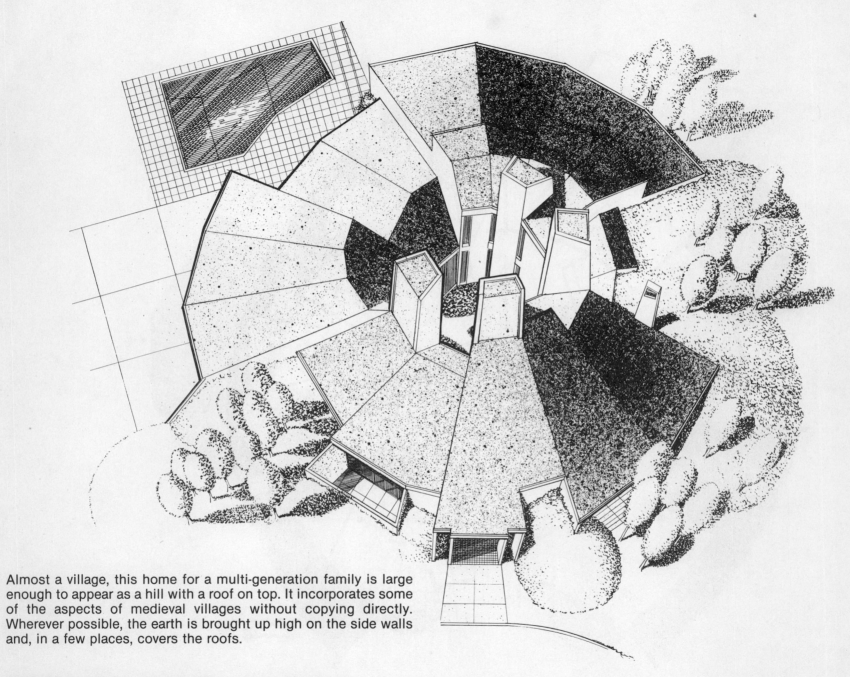

Almost a village, this home for a multi-generation family is large enough to appear as a hill with a roof on top. It incorporates some of the aspects of medieval villages without copying directly. Wherever possible, the earth is brought up high on the side walls and, in a few places, covers the roofs.

RADIATING PLAN — 5,800 S.F.

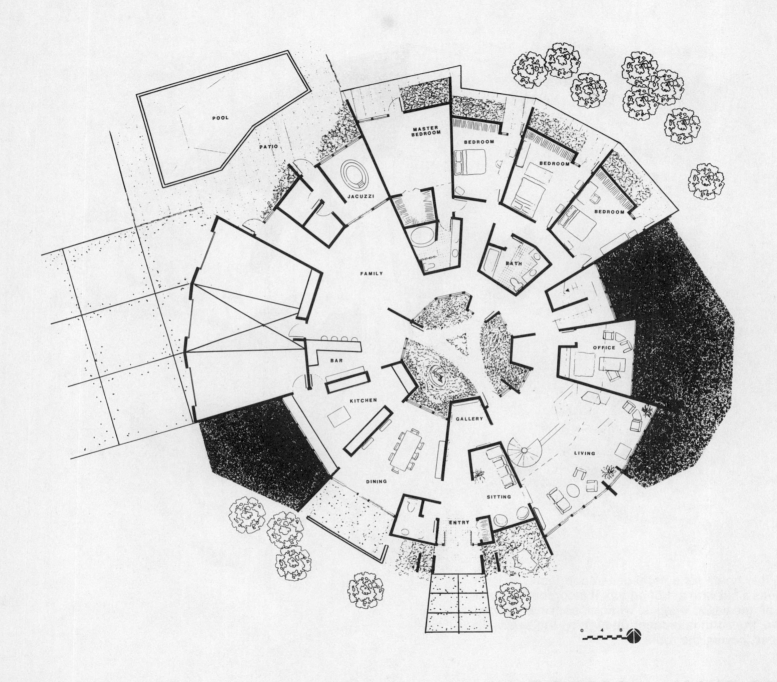

POOL

PATIO

JACUZZI

MASTER BEDROOM

BEDROOM

BEDROOM

BEDROOM

FAMILY

BATH

OFFICE

BAR

KITCHEN

GALLERY

LIVING

DINING

SITTING

ENTRY

0 4 8